Is Black Anger Justified?
Inspired by NFL Protests

Highlighting Personal Experiences,
Current Events, and History

WAYNE PERRYMAN

BOOK PUBLISHERS NETWORK
Changing the World One Book at a Time

Book Publishers Network
P.O. Box 2256
Bothell • WA • 98041
Ph • 425-483-3040
www.bookpublishersnetwork.com

10 9 8 7 6 5 4 3 2 1
Printed in the United States of America

LCCN   2018940575
ISBN   978-1-945271-97-7

Wall Street Journal Rights Link Printable License.pdf Information Case #00459336 - Permission to Reprint Wall Street Journal August 18, 2014 Article

Cover Art & Design by Mike Fox | Splash Designworks LLC

Wayne Perryman
P.O. Box 256
Mercer Island, WA 98040
doublebro@aol.com

Be ye angry and sin not

Ephesian 4:26 (King James)

Contents

Introduction

Anger? Many whites ask: *Why would a black minister write a book about angry black people? Aren't blacks always angry?* I'm writing this book not only to highlight my personal experiences as an African American father but also to show how these common, everyday experiences in the lives of African Americans produce the justified anger that our white colleagues often complain about. Anger is justified but not if it is used to harm yourself or others.

Like me, it is highly unlikely that any African American (male or female) has not experienced some form of racism during his or her lifetime because of the color of his or her skin, whether the experience was:

A. being watched and followed around the store while shopping;
B. being watched by police or residents in predominately white neighborhoods;
C. overhearing racial jokes and comments about blacks;
D. being part of negative stereotypes about African Americans;
E. being denied employment, loans, or promotional opportunities;
F. being a victim of the criminal justice system;
G. being denied educational opportunities;
H. being falsely accused of some action;
I. being alienated simply because of race;
J. being treated like a second-class citizen in restaurants, hotels, or retail outlets;
K. having issues with housing and where you can or cannot live;
L. denial of membership in various groups or organizations;
M. racially biased reporting by the news media;
N. being ignored while waiting for service;

O. being accused of using ***the race card*** for his or her benefit and to condemn whites;

P. being stopped by the police for DWB (driving while black);

Q. having his or her children alienated at school during recess;

R. his or her community not receiving the same public services as other neighborhoods;

S. not being believed when responding to questions by authorities;

T. having lower quality of products to choose from in neighborhood stores;

U. homes devalued because he or she lives in a predominately black community;

V. not having quality health care available in the area where he or she lives;

W. having his or her problems ignored by politicians;

X. being complimented for his or her speech for not sounding black;

Y. having to participate in public protest just to be heard; or

Z. whites choosing not to get on the elevator because too many blacks were on the elevator.

It seems like these types of incidents never end. In less than thirty days in 2018 the following incidents occurred:

1. April 18, 2018 – Starbucks' CEO, Kevin Johnson apologized to two African American young men who were arrested simply because they were sitting in the Starbucks Store waiting to meet someone.

2. May 7, 2018 – A white student at Yale University called the police to report that a black female was sleeping in the common room at Yale's Graduate Studies building. After arriving at the scene the police learned that the black female was a grad-student and lived in the resident and was tired from studies.

3. May 9, 2018 – Nordstrom's President, Geevy Thomas apologized to three African American teens who were falsely accused of shoplifting after being followed around

the store by Nordstrom employees. The young men like many students during this time of the year, were shopping for clothing to wear at the Prom.

Black Survival Skills

Like a mother bear or a mother lion, who teaches her cubs how to survive in the wild, black children are taught how to survive in a racist society by their parents and members in their community. Survival information includes:

1. Staying out of gangs
2. Staying away from drugs
3. Going to school
4. Watching out for bad influences
5. Being careful of white police officers
6. Being aware of double standards because of the color of their skin

Most of our survival skills require careful observations. *Watch out for this. Watch out for that.* In the 2017-2018 school year, black children as young as five years old have reported that white children on school buses or during recess either called them "niggers" or told the black child that they "are not allowed to sit next to them." Interesting! That's exactly what they told my bi-racial son twenty years ago while riding on a school bus and exactly what they told blacks in the Jim Crow South some sixty years ago when they forced Rosa Parks and other blacks to sit in the back of the bus. The little children who were called "nigger" did not fully understand the context and/or the origin of the negative term; they just knew that it was wrong for whites to use language like that toward African Americans. In other words, the survival instincts that were instilled in them kicked in when they were called "nigger."

Those That Didn't Survive

In 2012, when Lebron James, Dwayne Wade, and the other members of the Miami Heat NBA basketball team came out during pre-game warm ups wearing hoodies, they did so to protest the death of Trayvon Martin. It was one of the first times that a group of black athletes (since the 1968 Olympics) stood together to express their anger for the injustices that young black men experience every day. When they launched their quiet protest, little did they know that Trayvon's death would be followed by the death of other unarmed black men like Freddy Gray, Eric Garner, Tamir Rice, Philando Castile, Laquan McDonald, and Terence Crutcher.

Eric Garner: The nation watched as several New York police officers choked Eric Garner (an unarmed black man) to death as he consistently cried out, "I can't breathe." The police stopped Garner because it was reported that he was selling unauthorized cigarettes.

Tamir Rice was a twelve-year-old boy in Cleveland playing with a toy gun near a park when two police officers shot him within "two seconds" after they arrived at the scene.

Philando Castile of Minnesota, a well-liked school employee, was shot to death while sitting in his car next to his girlfriend. Castile was stopped because of a broken taillight. Prior to the killing, he informed the police that he had a gun in the car (and a permit to carry it) and that he was reaching for his license not a gun. The police stood just outside of the driver's side window and shot him several times, as he complied with the officer's command to give him his license.

Laquan McDonald, a seventeen-year-old Chicago teenager, was captured on the police cam walking down the middle of the street unarmed when a police officer shot him sixteen times as he was walking away from the officer.

Terence Crutcher, of Tulsa, Oklahoma, was shot to death while his hands were raised walking toward his SUV. The female officer who shot him was acquitted even though Mr. Crutcher was unarmed and showed no aggressive movement toward the officer. From shootings and harassments to racial profiling and false arrests, the Department of Justice announced in 2017 that it was investigating 20 different police departments for "discriminatory policing." In several police jurisdictions across the country, African American men still face the old Jim Crow style policing of yesterday.

Stephon Clark was the latest victim. Clark was a 22-year-old California father of two who was unarmed when police shot at him 20 times on March 18, 2018. He was hit eight times, an independent autopsy shows. Mr. Clark received seven gunshot wounds in his back. An eighth bullet hit Clark in the arm.

History of Blacks & White Police Officers

In my studies, I learned that the first law enforcement officers in the South where 98 percent of African Americans resided were individuals who were known as the slave patrols, a group that was formed in the 1700s to capture runaway slaves. After slavery and during Reconstruction and the Jim Crow era, the slave patrols remained intact and became the law of the land enforcing laws to keep blacks in their place and to punish those who were considered "uppity niggers." Many of these white police officers were members of the Ku Klux Klan. When the South first started hiring black officers (in the 1940s and 1950s), black officers could not patrol in white neighborhoods. Most of the crimes (including mass murder) committed against blacks by white citizens and white police officers resulted in no arrests, no charges, and no prosecutions.

Today's police officers must realize that just because a person is wrapped in black skin, does not (automatically) make him or her a criminal, and blacks must realize just because a person is white wearing a blue uniform with a badge, does not (automatically) make him or her a racist. The difference between black citizens and white police officers is the three-hundred-year history (since 1704) of racist practices by white police officers against blacks but there is no history of blacks trying to harm police officers simply because they are white.

Exploring Black Anger

Now let us explore both current events and events of the past that makes blacks angry. In our exploration, you will find that black history is a very ugly history, but out of the ugliness came beautiful expressions of compassion, kindness and caring as demonstrated in chapters 8 and 9. Our exploration will start with the treatment of young black men, today and yesterday.

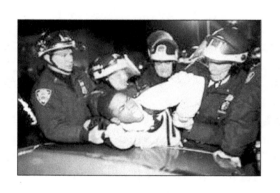

Chapter 1

False Arrests and Investigations
of Young Black Men

Injustice anywhere is a threat to justice everywhere.
– Dr. Martin Luther King Jr.

Besides Emmett Till, one of the saddest cases of racial injustice in American history was the Kalief Browder case. It is a case about a black teenager who was falsely accused, arrested and imprisoned for three years for a crime that he never committed. During his incarceration, prison videos showed that he was abused and beaten and spent a large portion of the three years in solitary confinement. After proving he was innocent and was finally released, he eventually committed suicide. Browder could not get rid of the nightmares from his experiences during imprisonment, and because of his arrest record, he could not get a decent job. Browder was arrested for stealing a backpack, something that had little value and one that he never stole or had possession of (see the Netflix documentary, *Time: The Kalief Browder Story*). The false arrest destroyed him, as it is doing to a number of African American males today.

It matters not if you are a young black man who never finished high school like Kalief Browder or a college honor student like Sean Perryman. If you are a black male, in the eyes of far too many white police officers, you are likely to be a criminal. What Browder and Perryman had in common is they both were black, innocent, arrested, and charged with a crime they did not commit. But unlike Browder, Perryman had a well-known supportive black father who loved him, stood by him, and fought for him. On April 4, 2015 when Perryman (my son) went out with a few white friends on that Easter weekend, he was unaware that in 2012, US Attorney Jenny Durkan of the Department of Justice (under the auspices of Attorney General Eric Holder) had filed a class action lawsuit against the Seattle Police Department for "discriminatory policing."

On April 8, 2015, Detective Paul Suguro of the Seattle Police Department completed and submitted Case Investigation Report No. 2015-109387 in support of his third-degree assault charge against Sean Christian Perryman (see appendix 1). Sworn under the penalty of perjury of the State of Washington, Detective Suguro reported the following:

> There was a disturbance in front of the Rhino Room involving Matthew Taylor and security guards from the Rhino Room. Taylor's friend, Sean Christian Perryman, tried to calm Taylor down. [Justin] Ismael saw Perryman throw Taylor to the ground. Ismael intervene[d] in an attempt to calm down Taylor and Perryman. Witnesses [white security guards and Ismael's white friend] said Perryman shoved Ismael, pushing him to ground. Perryman [an African American] started attacking Ismael by punching and kicking Ismael. Rhino Room security guards were able to separate Perryman from Ismael and handcuffed Perryman. Seattle Police arrived. Ismael identified Perryman to the officers and the one who pushed him to the ground and attacked him.

Based solely on the testimonies of three white witnesses (Rhino Security manager James Hargen, bystander Justin Ismael, and Ismael's friend Michael Davis), the Seattle Police placed Perryman under arrest and charged him with assault. They did so without ever reviewing the video from the Rhino Room's sixteen surveillance cameras to determine whether the white witnesses were telling the truth. After personally reviewing the surveillance video, King County prosecutor, Dan Satterberg, dismissed all charges against Perryman, and in a private meeting with me, he issued an apology for how the police handled the situation. Not only did this nightmare experience cause Sean much anxiety and many sleepless nights wondering how all this would affect his future, it also forced me to borrow a significant amount of money to hire one of the best defense lawyers to represent my son.

Details of the Racially Biased Police Investigation
The following information is taken from surveillance video, police reports, police cams, and court briefs.

On April 4, 2015, there was an incident at Rhino Room bar in which the Civil Rights of Matthew Taylor, a white young man and Sean Christian Perryman, an African American young man were violated by the Seattle Police Department and the Rhino Room personnel. The incident occurred on the sidewalk outside the Rhino Bar located at Eleventh Avenue and Pine Street in Seattle, Washington.

The evening started when Matthew Taylor, Sean C. Perryman, and another friend decided to go to the Rhino Bar late Friday evening on April 3, 2015 (Easter weekend). Upon arrival, they all paid the same cover charge and the Rhino Bar gave the two white patrons a color wristband indicating they had paid, but for some reason they did not do the same for Perryman. He received no wristband. At the time, the three young men thought nothing of this disparity, a disparity that would later set in motion the arrest of Sean Christian Perryman and the denial of due process for Matthew Taylor.

As the night progressed, Perryman wanted to step outside for some fresh air. The surveillance video shows that he started out but changed his mind and never passed the doorway. A plain-clothes Rhino security guard followed Perryman back inside and demanded that he leave. When Taylor, Perryman's friend, learned what happened, he came to Perryman's defense and informed the security guard that they all came together and all paid the same cover charge and questioned why they would not allow Perryman to re-enter when they were allowing whites patrons to re-enter.

Taylor became uncontrollably angry and repeatedly "protested" their policy, which seemed to be racist. His constant nagging aggravated the door security guard. The two began to have a heated exchange. At exactly 1:14:27 a.m., the surveillance video shows Justin Ismael and his friend Michael Davis coming out of the bar. Ismael immediately engaged in the dispute on the side of the security guards. No one knew who he was and why he chose to involve himself in the dispute between Taylor and the security personnel. As Detective Suguro's Police Report correctly reported, "Perryman tried to calm Taylor down" several times, often picking him up and carrying him down the street only to see Taylor return. Perryman eventually told Taylor he was not interested in re-entering and to forget the entire matter and said, "Let's go home." Taylor continued to argue with the security guard and threatened to file a complaint against the Rhino Bar.

During the heated exchange with the guards, Taylor took out his cell phone camera to take a photo of the security guard (the guards were wearing street clothes, not formal uniforms). At 1:14:59 a.m., the surveillance video shows that one of the guards snatched Taylor's cell phone. At 1:15:48 a.m., the video shows another guard quietly positioning himself behind Taylor on the public sidewalk. When Taylor grabbed his phone and attempted to take the photo, the guard on the public sidewalk attacked Taylor from behind knocking him to the pavement and proceeded to punch him several times in the head (recorded at 1:17:36 a.m.). Taylor was standing on the public sidewalk when the attack occurred. When Perryman intervened to rescue Taylor by merely pushing the guard away (at 1:17:40 a.m.), two other plain-clothes security guards, Justin Ismael and Michael Davis, "rushed" to attack Perryman, eventually throwing him into on-coming traffic, driving his face into the concrete, busting his lips, chipping his teeth, using both a choke hold and a Taser to stop him from defending himself and protecting Taylor. The surveillance video clearly shows that Ismael was the aggressor and that he injured himself when he aggressively went after Perryman. During his aggressive attack, Ismael fell awkwardly and dislocated his knee, and for this, the police charged Perryman with third degree assault.

Taylor got up and called 911 to report that he had just been assaulted. While talking to the 911 operator, one security guard continued to pursue Taylor as heard on the 911 call. Taylor told the operator that the security guards were on top of Perryman with his face pinned to the ground and that he was spitting out blood. The police precinct, which was only one block away, responded with a total of eight police officers. When the police refused to accept Taylor's version of what happened, Taylor told the officer, "Look at the video if you don't believe me.". The police ignored his recommendation and put their focus on Perryman and Ismael's injury, while the medics attended to Taylor's injuries.

Without interviewing any of the bystanders who saw the entire incident, video taped the incident and shouted "what are you doing? He didn't do nothing" [much like the bystanders in the Starbucks incident in Philadelphia], the police chose to interview only James Hargen (security manager), Justin Ismael, and Ismael's friend, Michael

Davis, the three who were involved in the incident. Their version of what took place was contradicted by a surveillance video that the police chose not to review at the crime scene. As reported in the police report, the security guards told the police that Perryman tried to calm Taylor down, and then, all of a sudden (for no reason), Perryman attacked (his own friend) Taylor, throwing Taylor to the ground. When Ismael came to Taylor's rescue, Perryman turned and attacked Ismael by throwing Ismael to the ground and started "kicking and punching" him (which dislocated his knee). The surveillance video shows that this *never* happened. Without checking the video from two of the sixteen surveillance cameras that captured the eight-second altercation and clearly showed that Perryman never attacked Taylor, never pushed Ismael to the ground, and never punched him or kicked him, the police ignored the video and arrested Perryman and charged him with assault. Four days later (April 8, 2012), Detective Suguro completed his investigation and submitted his report to the King County prosecutor for prosecution.

Acting on a tip from Perryman's father, attorney Robert Flennaugh demanded a copy of the surveillance video. On April 15, 2012 (eleven days later), Detective Surguro sent an officer to the Rhino Bar to obtain the video (see appendix 1). The surveillance video totally contradicted the witnesses' version of what happened. The video showed that the three white witnesses had deliberately and intentionally fabricated their story to have Perryman arrested, a story that the Seattle Police chose not to verify at the crime scene. The eight white police officers seemed more interested in arresting Perryman (the only black person involved), rather than one of the eight officers taking eight seconds (out of their twenty-eight minutes at the crime scene) to look at the video to see what really happened. Additionally, the police chose not to arrest the white security guard who initiated the physical fight by attacking Taylor from behind, punching him several times in the head, and chasing him while he (Taylor) was talking to the 911 operator. This individual was never arrested, even though Taylor told the police that he wanted to press charges against him (three times on the police cam).

After obtaining a copy of the surveillance video, the King County prosecutor apologized and dismissed the case. The police never modified, revised, or corrected their police reports to reflect what the video actually showed and never apologized for the arrest. In fact, the detective in charge of the investigation kept the video in his personal possession and never entered it as evidence until two weeks after the case was dismissed (much like the detective in the OJ case who kept a sample of OJ's blood in his personal possession and took it home with him). See appendix 1.

From a Reputation of Kindness to a Criminal

Prior to his arrest, Sean Perryman had an impeccable record. He was on the dean's list in college, was a member of the National Society of Collegiate Scholars, had received scholarships for outstanding character, helped the underprivileged, was an author at the age of fourteen, and when he learned there was a project to dig clean water wells in Africa for small children, he donated his life savings (intended for a car) to the project. Additionally, I had trained police departments (but not the Seattle Police Department) in the area of race relations. Now Sean had an arrest record that will follow him for the rest of his life. Not just any type of an arrest record, but an arrest record for a violent crime, one that is currently showing up on background-check websites (see appendix 2). The court acknowledged that three white witnesses lied to have Sean Perryman arrested for a crime he did not commit, which is an obstruction of justice and violates RCW 9A.76.175 for intentionally lying to public authorities. But the three white individuals were never charged or arrested.

Because Perryman's arrest for assault remains in police files (with no corrections), his record will appear on police car computers every time he is stopped for a traffic violation. The record will suggest that he is potentially a violent person and a possible threat, which means the police should be very cautious and watch his every move. Whether innocent or guilty, a black man with an arrest record, according to criminal justice experts, is a signed death certificate to his future.

Perryman filed a civil suit to clear his name and to recover legal expenses. The civil lawsuit is scheduled for July 2, 2018, in Seattle's federal court.

Chapter 2

The Devastation of Incarceration
and Arrest Records

Black Men with Arrest Records

Because of the witnesses' false statements and the police's racially biased investigation, Sean Perryman now faces an uncertain future with an arrest record for a crime he did not commit. In today's world of internet background checks, the best way to destroy a black male's life (and his future) is simply to arrest him. Arrests for African American males can be devastating. The following studies shows that the devastation of incarceration is almost irrevocable even if you are found not guilty of the crime you are charged with:

On August 20, 2014, **the Justice Center of the Council of State Governments** published an article entitled: "Researcher Examine Effects of Criminal Record on Prospects of Employment." The article says:

> A team of researchers from Arizona State University recently conducted a three-year study on the impact of having a criminal record on employment related outcomes, varying by race and gender. The research included 6,000 applicants in three job sectors, including customer service, general/manual labor and restaurant/food service. Their research reveal how arrests records can harm black males: "Both Black and Hispanic men were less likely to receive a positive response from employers—including a call back or email for an interview or a job offer compared to white men."

Dr. Gwen Sharp cites a study conducted by Dr. Devah Pager on "preferred job applicants." In that study, Dr. Sharp says, "Getting a job with a criminal record is difficult. Having even a non-violent drug offense had a significant impact on rates of callbacks. African Americans with a non-violent offense faced particularly dismal employment prospects." She goes on to say:

> Imagine if the person had a property or a violent crime arrest.

Employers seem to expect that Black applicants might have a criminal record. When people think of Black men they think of a criminal. It affects the way Black men are treated in the labor market. In fact, Black testers in our study were likely to be asked up front if they have a criminal record, while whites were rarely asked. African American men face a double barrier; higher rates of incarceration and racial discrimination.

In discussing background investigations, Joe Kelly in the July 2012 *Tennessee Labor and Employment Newsletter* wrote:

CNN reports that 79% of all businesses use the Internet to investigate job applicants. A recent poll revealed that 70% of hiring managers have said they have rejected a job applicant based on information they found online.

In the *Wall Street Journal* article of August 18, 2014, entitled "As Arrest Records Rise, Americans Find Consequences Can Last a Lifetime," Gary Fields and John R. Emshwiller say:

An information explosion has made it easy for anyone to pull up arrest records in an instant. Employers, banks, college administration officers and landlords, among others routinely check records on online. The information doesn't typically describe what happened next.

Many people who have never faced charges, or have had charges dropped find that a lingering arrest record can ruin their chance to secure employment loans, and housing. Even if in cases of mistaken arrest, the information is forwarded to the FBI but not necessarily updated when a case is thrown out locally. Only half of the records with the FBI have fully up-to-date information. "There is a myth that if you are arrested and cleared that it has no impact," says Paul Butler, professor of law at Georgetown Law. "It's not like it never happened."

Exacerbating the situation are for-profit websites and other background-check businesses that assemble publicly available arrest records, records that often included mug shots and out dated charges. Many sites charge fees to remove records, even outdated or erroneous one. In the past year Google Inc. has changed its search algorithm to de-emphasize many so-called "mug-shots" website, giving them less prominence when someone's name is searched (see appendix 3 for the complete Wall Street Journal article).

The growing obsession with background checking and commercial exploitation of arrest and convictions records makes it all but impossible for someone with a criminal record to leave the past behind, concludes a recent report from the National Association of Criminal Defense Lawyers.

Further analysis by the University of South Carolina team, performed at the request of the Wall Street Journal, suggest that men with arrest records—even absent a formal charge or conviction—go on to earn lower salaries. They are also less likely to own a home compared with people who have never been arrested.

Amended Civil Rights Equal Employment Laws now allow employers to use arrest records to deny individuals employment. (See appendix 3.) The Equal Employment Opportunity Commission reports:

The question addressed in this policy guidance is "to what extent may arrest records be used in making employment decisions?" . . . Where it appears that the applicant or employee engaged in conduct for which he was arrested and that the conduct is job-related and relatively recent, exclusion is justified. . . .

. . . Blacks and Hispanics are convicted in numbers which are disproportionate to Whites and that barring people from employment based on their conviction records will therefore disproportionately exclude those groups. Due to this adverse impact, an employer may not base an employment decision on the conviction record of an applicant or employee absent of business necessity. Business necessity can be established where the employee or applicant is engaged in conduct which is particularly egregious or related to the position in question [arrest for assaults can be considered egregious].

On February 28, 2015, in an article entitled: "Out of Trouble, but Criminal Records Keep Men Out of Work" *New York Times*, Reporter Binyamin Appelbaum reported that the number of black men with criminal records has increased during the past few decades, and as a result, it is very difficult for African American young men to become productive members of society. Most employers, banks, and various other institutions use online background checks to investigate everyone. See background check on Sean Perryman, Appendix 2.

Chapter 3

Bias-Free Professional Standards for Police Investigations

According to the International Association of Chiefs of Police (IACP), very few police (including the Seattle Police) follow the procedures recommended by the IACP for investigating crimes (this is particularly true in crimes involving black suspects). The IACP agrees that innocent people are convicted because of "eyewitnesses misidentification, lying informants and faulty investigative thinking." Further, it says:

> When investigations are not conducted properly innocent persons are convicted. . . If a police officer has limited or incorrect information [from lying witnesses], their starting point will be wrong. . . . One of the leading causes of wrongful convictions [and arrests] results from a narrow focus on a limited range of possibilities. . . If alternative theories to the crime are not considered, potential suspects are eliminated from the investigation. . .

> Focusing on the first likely suspect, and then closing the investigation off to alternative theories, is a recipe for disaster.

> Sometimes the most prestigious law enforcement agencies are the most reluctant to admit mistakes. But truth is more important than reputation. An investigator must have the flexibility to admit his or her original theory was incorrect.

In addition to not following the investigative procedures, the Seattle Police did not follow the recommended standards of the International Association of Chiefs of Police regarding relying on available surveillance videos as part of their investigations. In *The Police Chief*, the official magazine of the IACP, Grant Fredericks writes an article entitled: "CCTV: A Law Enforcement Tool," he states the following regarding the importance of surveillance cameras and videos in police investigation:

A crime scene is just where the search begins when looking for video that may assist an investigation. A sharp-eyed investigator can survey businesses or public buildings near the scene and spot the tell-take smoked plastic domes concealing the cameras that might have caught a suspect fleeing the area.

Video evidence often provides the investigator with the first glimpse of the crime, giving the investigator a virtual and contemporary walk-through of the crime scene as the event took place. Confident but overzealous witnesses who might otherwise lead an investigation down the wrong path can be easily discounted and more valuable witnesses are prioritized as their observations more accurately reflect the actual events recorded to tape.

Video and audio evidence can be among the most compelling exhibits a prosecutor can present at trial.

Because many police departments choose not to follow these recommended investigative procedures, many young African American men are falsely arrested, charged, and convicted of crimes they did not commit (the Browder and Perryman cases are prime examples of police ignoring video evidence).

Department of Justice Investigation of Seattle Police

Mayor Jenny Durkan, the former lead US attorney who filed the suit against the Seattle Police in 2012 (see appendix 4), stated that the Department of Justice's "Investigation of the Seattle Police Department" included reviewing:

> hundreds of thousands of pages of documents, including SPD's written policies and procedures; its training materials; its internal use of force reports; SPD and OPA [Office of Professional Accountability]'s public reports; OPA's complaints and investigative files; and data generated from SPD and OPA data bases. The data included hundred hours of video footage. . . .

... Our investigation identified three systemic deficiencies that contribute to the problem that SPD should
correct: (a) the failure to adequately collect data necessary to assess allegations of discriminatory policing; ...
... our investigation raises serious concerns about
practices *that could have a disparate impact on minority
communities.*

The complaint (*United States of America v. City of Seattle*) filed
by Durkan and Thomas Perez on July 26, 2012, about the Seattle
Police Department (SPD) stated:

The City has spent millions of dollars in attorney's
fees defending police misconduct cases. In the last six
years, it has paid approximately $3 million in settle-
ments, verdicts and attorney's fees to plaintiffs. ...
In short, SPD knew or should have known that its
policies and practices...would inevitably cause Fourth
Amendment violations. ...
... For years, the SPD disposed of nearly two-thirds
of citizens' complaints by sending them to SPD's precincts, where the quality of investigation is deficient.

Mayor Durkan's Investigation

Several citizens, including a retired police officer, have asked
Mayor Durkan to look into the Sean Perryman case and the Police
Department that she had previously investigated and has inherited.
As of the date of this publication, there are no reports or updates re-
garding her investigation (see appendix 4). How will she respond?
Given the fact that blacks and whites can look at the same evidence
and reach different opinions and conclusions, no one knows how she
will respond. She is white, and Sean Perryman is black.

Many whites reject the idea that whites form opinions based on
race, that is until a black tries to move into their neighborhood and/
or until they are forced to face a black person in court. In court cases
(like the OJ case), white attorneys will do everything possible to keep
blacks off the jury. In the movie *A Time to Kill*, actor Samuel Jackson

tells his white lawyer, "I picked you because you are one of them and think like them" (meaning the white jury). Not only do blacks and whites see things differently based on their life experience, women and men also view things differently through their gender experiences. A person's race, gender, life experiences, and/or background are factors that are considered in jury selections. This was one of the concerns of the parents of the UCLA basketball players who were arrested in China for shoplifting and the concerns of the friends of Amanda Knox who was arrested and tried for murder in Italy. In both cases, the individuals were arrested by the authorities of that country, they were to be prosecuted by the prosecutors of that country, and the judge and the jury of that country would decide their fate. In the OJ civil trial, the plaintiff 's attorney preferred "white women or abused women" as opposed to black jurors. Nicole Simpson's attorneys requested and were granted a change of venue, they preferred a county where the jury pool would have fewer African Americans.

White elected officials like Mayor Durkan (and/or white judges) feel their legal training makes them color blind and their decisions will be based solely on the law, rather than their personal life experiences or stereotypical opinions. Every study shows this is not the case, whether the judge is black or white. *The Oxford Companion to the Supreme Court of the United States* (produced by over four hundred legal scholars) states:

> The opinion of the Court [in the court's Dred Scott's decision] was shaped by a variety of factors. The most obvious was the *attitudes* [emphasis added] of the individual justices. Of the nine justices, five were appointed by legislators that supported slavery and four were from slaveholding states.

During the past three hundred years, rarely have there ever been cases involving African Americans where the judge was not white, the prosecutor was not white, and the jury was not white or mostly white. It is almost impossible for the average white person (based on his or her experience) to think like African Americans or feel the pain of blacks. This is not an indictment against whites; it is just a fact, and it applies to all persons with different life experiences. Most African Americans do not think like blacks from Haiti, India, Brazil, and the many war-torn countries in Africa because their experiences are different. It is our experience that shapes the way we think. This was best illustrated in the movie: *The 12 Angry Men*, starring Henry Fonda. The twelve men that made up the jury, struggled in deciding the fate (of what appeared to be) a Puerto Rican young man on trial for murder, while they wrestled with their own personal attitudes and prejudices. As The *Oxford Companion* said, it was the Supreme Court Justices' "attitudes" that influenced and shaped their decision in many cases involving African Americans, not the law. Five of them were put on the court by legislators that supported slavery, and other four were from slaveholding states.

It is very difficult for the average white person to believe that a black arrested for a crime is innocent, even if there is video evidence to prove that he did not commit the crime. In both the Browder case and the Perryman case, the videos clearly showed that these two black men did not commit the crime they were charged with, and yet they were still arrested, incarcerated, and charged by white police officers, based on the false testimonies of white witnesses. Despite the video evidence, it has taken the mayor of Seattle (who happens to be white) several weeks to determine whether the police should have looked at the video before arresting Perryman (a black man). In contrast, it took the black attorneys in the Prosecutor's Office just minutes after viewing the video (as part of their investigation) to reach the decision that Perryman was innocent and never should have been arrested. Until whites accept the fact that their opinions of blacks are shaped by stereotypes and their own personal experiences, improving race relations will be virtually impossible. The problem with the black experience is that the painful events of the past—such as false arrests, the killing of unarmed black men by authorities, disparities in the criminal justice system, and discrimination in employment and housing—keep recurring.

Emotionally Detached from Blacks
Why did the black female attorneys in the Prosecutor's Office respond much quicker than the white mayor (who is also an attorney and has yet to respond)? Anytime you are emotionally detached from

a person's or a group's painful experience, it will be very difficult to relate to them, respond to them, or understand them. (See appendix 10, "List of Abolitionists," and chapter 9, "Embracing Our White Allies.")

We all (black and white) had an emotional attachment with the parents who lost their children at Sandy Hook Elementary School in Newtown, Connecticut, on December 14, 2012, and we had an emotional attachment with the parents of the seventeen high school students who lost their lives in the South Florida killings on Valentine's Day 2018, but America has yet to have an emotional attachment with the painful black experience. Many say the shooters in each of the aforementioned incidents had issues of mental illness. African Americans believe that *racism* is also a mental illness.

The bottom line is this: it is hard to understand persons that you are not emotionally connected with or cannot identify with. The black prosecuting attorneys (with very large caseloads) in the Perryman case not only had knowledge of the law and the evidence; they were also emotionally sensitive to the reality that black men from time to time are falsely accused. In contrast, it appears that as mayor, Durkan too had the same evidence and knowledge of the law but apparently lacked what the black attorneys have—the emotional connection with innocent black men who are falsely accused and an understanding of the damage it can do to their future. As a US attorney, for five years (from 2012 to 2018), dealing with "discriminatory policing" within the Seattle Police Department was Durkan's top priority. As mayor this issue is no longer a priority. She and other elected officials apparently forgot the words of Rev. Dr. Martin Luther King Jr. when he said: "Injustice anywhere is a threat to justice everywhere." When he spoke these words, he was speaking to those in authority who had the power to address racial discrimination.

Final note: It is difficult to believe that America can identify with African Americans' pains of injustice when we see football stadiums, baseball stadiums, basketball arenas, corporations, and municipal buildings flying flags of other groups during their appropriate time of recognition but never fly our flag during Black History Month. During the past forty-two years, cities and counties across the country have planned and budgeted for Black History celebrations. On February 22, 2018, black police officers of the Seattle Police Department invited me to be the keynote speaker for the City of Seattle's Black History Month celebration at the Seattle police's headquarters. Mayor Durkan and the city council did not attend. It was reported by the officers that the city had no budget for the Black History celebration, so many of the officers financed the event themselves. Only three or four white police officers attended (Seattle Police has over 1200 officers). Black police officers reported that it is mandatory for them to take an eight hour training course on the Holocaust, but the same is not required for black history or black culture.

It is not my intention to indict all white people. There are a number of wonderful, thoughtful white Americans as pointed out in chapter 9, "Embracing Our White Allies," and in eleven pages of appendix 10. It is the hypocritical ones who pretend to be something they are not who are the problem, like the NFL and its hypocritical past relationship with our military.

Chapter 4

The NFL and Respect for Soldiers

NFL Makes Military Pay

Whites fans and NFL owners complained that our black ball players were disrespecting our soldiers when they knelt during the playing of the national anthem before the game, but the owners kept silent when the media reported that fourteen teams in the NFL charged the military $5.4 million dollars just to be on the field for "The Star-Spangled Banner" and to place military advertisements on the jumbo screens in the stadiums (see appendix 7). When the NFL was finally exposed, New Jersey senator Joe Pennachhio said, "If these teams want to really honor our veterans and service members they should be making these patriotic overtures out of gratitude for free, and the millions of dollars that they have already been billed to taxpayers should be donated to veteran organizations." Most fans did not know that the Defense Department was funneling taxpayer money into the NFL in exchange for veteran tributes. Those who did know kept silent, refused to condemn the NFL and chose instead to join the owners in condemning the black NFL players who chose to kneel.

NFL Fans and Disrespect for Black Soldiers

Most whites who believe NFL players are disrespecting the flag and the soldiers who fought and died for it when they kneel during "The Star-Spangled Banner" seldom ever think about the significant role that black soldiers played in every American war, from the Revolutionary War to our current conflicts in the Middle East. Because our black soldiers have never received the recognition due to them by white America, it is difficult for blacks to believe the celebration of the flag and "The Star-Spangled Banner "includes them.

Briefly, history reports that the first person to die for the freedom of our country was Crispus Attucks, a black man, during the Revolutionary War. Lincoln said the North never would have won the Civil War without the 180,000 brave black soldiers. During War World I and World War II, despite the fact that they were forced to fight in a segregated army, black soldiers in France (during World War I and the Tuskegee Airmen in America during World War II) were highly decorated by the millitary for their skills, their bravery, and the significant role they played in these wars.

When the white soldiers came home, America proudly stood at attention with their hands over their heart as the band played "The Star-Spangled Banner." The white soldiers then celebrated and enjoyed the same freedoms and benefits that they had enjoyed before they left for the war. When the white soldiers came home, they were able to get jobs, live where they wanted, sit anywhere on public transportation, eat in any restaurant, use better quality restrooms, drink in more sanitary drinking fountains, send their kids to any school or college they preferred, and work in the best jobs. But most of all, they weren't murdered, mutilated, decapitated, burned to death, lynched or forced to watch their communities burned to the ground like the black communities of Tulsa, Oklahoma, Wilmington, North Carolina, and Rosewood, Florida, simply because of the color of their skin. It was much different when blacks returned home after fighting for their country. When they returned home, they were treated like second-class citizens. Many were hanged, beaten, jailed, and told to *stay in their place*. The freedoms and the benefits that the white soldiers enjoyed were just a fantasy for the black soldiers.

Given the fact of how black soldiers were treated, black soldiers weren't dying for their own freedom—they died for the freedom of white Americans. When the black soldier came home, there were laws in many states specifically legislated to deny their families the same rights and benefits that their white counterparts enjoyed. Black soldiers as a whole were never recognized or appreciated by America for their tremendous heroic service to our country.

What is interesting is that in 2017, when President Trump made his statement regarding the white supremacist's protest in Charlottesville, high-ranking officers in every branch of the military immediately denounced racism. Why? Because these high-ranking officers knew the history of racism in the military and how dedicated black soldiers were treated in the military and how they were treated when they returned home. They knew these soldiers weren't the benefactors of the freedom that they fought for. They knew there were signs telling the black soldiers (when they returned home) to "stay in their place" and not to be "uppity niggers" because some had European white and Japanese girlfriends while overseas. President Truman was upset when he learned that two black soldiers and their pregnant wives were murdered when the soldiers returned home from the war simply because of the color of their skin. Truman went to the national NAACP Convention to denounce the brutal murders. Historians say he was the first U.S. president to speak at a NAACP national convention.

When NFL fans and owners say that professional athletes are disrespecting our servicemen and the flag when they kneel during the national anthem, they overlook the years of disrespect that black soldiers experienced before, during, and after the wars they have fought in for the United States.

As stated before, African Americans fought in every war from the Revolutionary War to the current conflicts in the Middle East. They fought in every war, but unlike their white counterparts, they weren't the benefactors of the rights and freedoms afforded to white Americans until the 1960s. In 1963, in a letter to Congress, President John F. Kennedy included the following in his appeal to Congress on behalf of the long ignored African Americans.

> . . . *The Negro's drive for justice, however, has not stood still—nor will it, it is now clear, until full equality is achieved. The growing and understandable dissatisfaction of Negro citizens with the present pace of desegregation, and their increased determination to secure for themselves the equality of opportunity and treatment to which they are rightfully entitled, have underscored what should already have been clear: the necessity of the Congress enacting this year-not only the measures already proposed-but also additional legislation providing legal remedies for the denial of certain individual rights.*
>
> *The venerable code of equity law commands "for every wrong, a remedy." But in too many communities, in too many parts of the country, wrongs are inflicted on Negro citizens for which no effective remedy at law is clearly and readily available. State and local laws may even affirmatively seek to deny the rights to which these citizens are fairly entitled—and this can result only in a decreased respect for the law and increased violations of the law.*

In the continued absence of Congressional action, too many State and local officials as well as business-men will remain unwilling to accord these rights to all citizens. Some local courts and local merchants may well claim to be uncertain of the law, while those merchants who do recognize the justice of the Negro's request (and I believe these constitute the great majority of merchants, North and South) will be fearful of being the first to move, in the face of official, customer, employee or competitive pressures. [Angry] Negroes, consequently, can be expected to continue increasingly to seek the vindication of these rights through organized direct action, with all its potentially explosive consequences, such as we have seen in Birmingham, in Philadelphia, in Jackson, in Boston, in Cambridge, Maryland, and in many other parts of the country.

In short, the result of continued Federal legislative inaction will be continued, if not increased, racial strife—causing the leadership on both sides to pass from the hands of reasonable and responsible men to the purveyors of hate and violence, endangering domestic tranquility, retarding our Nation's economic and social progress and weakening the respect with which the rest of the world regards us. No American, I feel sure, would prefer this course of tension, disorder and division—and the great majority of our citizens simply cannot accept it....

Two months later, Dr. King stood on the steps of the Lincoln Memorial and made this appealed to his country :

". . . My country, 'tis of thee, sweet land of liberty, of thee I sing. Land where my fathers died, land of the pilgrim's pride, from every mountainside, let freedom ring."

And if America is to be a great nation this must become true. So let freedom ring from the prodigious hilltops of New Hampshire. Let freedom ring from the

*mighty mountains of New York. Let freedom ring from
the heightening Alleghenies of Pennsylvania!*

*Let freedom ring from the snowcapped Rockies of
Colorado!*

*Let freedom ring from the curvaceous slopes of
California!*

*But not only that; let freedom ring from Stone
Mountain of Georgia!*

*Let freedom ring from Lookout Mountain of
Tennessee!*

*Let freedom ring from every hill and molehill of
Mississippi. From every mountainside, let freedom ring.*

*And when this happens, when we allow freedom
to ring, when we let it ring from every village and every
hamlet, from every state and every city, we will be able
to speed up that day when all of God's children, black
men and white men, Jews and Gentiles, Protestants
and Catholics, will be able to join hands and sing in the
words of the old Negro spiritual, "Free at last! free at
last! thank God Almighty, we are free at last!"*

When Dr. King made reference to the "land where my fathers
died," he was including those black soldiers who gave their lives for
this country. To voluntarily die for a country that denies you citizenship and equality, is the ultimate unprecedented expression of patriotism. When it comes to patriotism, this is what the NFL fans and
owners fail to acknowledge:

- Blacks participated in the **Revolutionary War**, but when
  the war was over, white soldiers rejoiced for their inde-
  pendence, while black soldiers wept because their people were still in bondage. It was after the Revolutionary
  War that the Constitutional Convention reached an
  agreement that blacks for legislative purposes would be
  considered as "*three fifths of a person.*"

- Blacks fought in the **Creek Indian War**, but when they
  returned home, Congress passed the Fugitive Slave

Law, and some of the soldiers were accused of being fugitive slaves and were sent to plantations.

- Blacks fought in the **War of 1812**, but when they came home, the United States Supreme Court said they would not be classified as people but the *"mere property of the slave master"* (the famous Dred Scott Case).

- Blacks fought in the **Mexican-American War**, but when returned home, they weren't considered citizens of the country that they had fought for; 98 percent of the members of their race were still slaves.

- In **the Civil War** 180,000 blacks fought but were paid less than their white counterparts. When they came home, they faced Jim Crow laws and Black Codes and were denied citizenship and the right to vote.

- Blacks fought in the **Spanish American War**. When they returned home, the United States Supreme Court sanctioned segregation with the approval of *Plessy v. Ferguson* and the *Slaughterhouse Case*. During this same period, for minor crimes, thousands of black men and black children were sent to Convict Lease Camps, which provided free labor for rich Southern businessmen.

- Over two hundred thousand blacks fought in **World War I**, and 171 black soldiers of the 369th Infantry Regiment received France's highest medals of honors. But when they came home, they were told to stay in their place. Members of their race were killed when they tried to vote. Others were terrorized by the nation's first terrorist group, the Ku Klux Klan, a group that burned them, beat them, bombed their churches, burned their communities to the ground, and historians say the Klan hanged over four thousand. When they hung Mary Turner's husband because they claimed he was plotting to kill his employer,

Mary promised to find the men who hung him and have them arrested and tried for murder. The angry men went to the home of Mary Turner, grabbed her, dragged her down the road, doused her clothes with kerosene, hung her, ignited her clothes, then shot her several times. Mary was nine months pregnant at the time. While hanging on the tree, the mob cut open her stomach and the baby spilled out to the ground and cried. The men crushed the baby's skull with the heels of their boots and left.

- Blacks fought in **World War II**, and as in the Civil War and World War I, white soldiers refused to fight side by side with them nor were they allowed to sleep in the same barracks. The courageous Tuskegee Airmen of the 332nd Fighter Group received high honors, but when they came home, their children were forced to go to segregated schools, their wives could not eat at lunch counters, the men were denied employment, their families could not live where they wanted, and many members of their race were denied constitutional rights. For 187 years (from 1773 to 1960), African Americans were never the benefactors of the freedoms that they fought for, the same freedoms that were afforded to white soldiers and the members of their race. Black soldiers did not fight and die to endorse racism, but racism is what they received. They fought for "one nation under God, indivisible, with liberty and justice for all." They received segregation, isolation, and injustice instead of "liberty and justice." Their mistreatment happened while the flag was waving and Americans stood with their hands over their heart and proudly sang "The Star-Spangled Banner."

So when NFL owners, President Trump, and NFL fans refer to the soldiers who died, are they just referring to the white soldiers who fought and died or are they referring to the black soldiers who were forced to fight in a segregated military and then had to fight segregation when they returned home just to have the same rights as the white soldiers?

Kneeling and "The Star-Spangled Banner"

"The Star-Spangled Banner" was written by Francis Scott Key on September 14, 1814, during the War of 1812. Mr. Key was an attorney. His family owned slaves. And as an attorney, he prosecuted slaves who were classified as fugitives (and later in life defended them). As a slave owner, he included a third verse in "The Star-Spangled Banner," which says: "No refuge could save the hireling and slave, From the terror of flight, or the gloom of the grave:" I am confident that when Francis Scott Key wrote the words "O'er the land of the free," he did not have black slaves in mind or any other race of people. His thoughts about blacks at that time, was expressed in the third verse of his poem when he wrote that the slave would not escape the "gloom of the grave." Despite his feelings about blacks, in 1931, 109 years later, Congress designated "The Star-Spangled Banner" as our nation's National Anthem.

Ironically, the Negro National Anthem, "Lift Every Voice and Sing," by James Weldon Johnson had been established twenty years earlier by the NAACP. Johnson was a black school principal, and his song had no negative statements about whites or America, nor did it disavow or disrespect the American flag.

While Ray Charles and most Americans proudly sing more than one verse of "America the Beautiful," America and NFL fans never sing the third verse of "The Star-Spangled Banner." Failing to acknowledge that this third verse exists angers blacks.

The NFL's Disrespect for the American Flag

The popular story says that on May 29, 1777, Betsy Ross was asked to sew the flag that we now call the American flag. She had previously done some sewing for George Washington. On June 14, 1923, Congress introduced Chapter 10 of the US Code to set standards to respect the flag. According to those standards, millions of Americans, along with the NFL and their fans, disrespect the flag at every game. The following is taken directly from Title 36, Chapter 10 of the US Code covering respect for the flag:

§176. Respect for flag

No disrespect should be shown to the flag of the United States of America; the flag should not be dipped to any person or thing. Regimental colors, State flags, and organization or institutional flags are to be dipped as a mark of honor.

(a) The flag should never be displayed with the union down, except as a signal of dire distress in instances of extreme danger to life or property.

(b) The flag should never touch anything beneath it, such as the ground, the floor, water, or merchandise.

(c) The flag should never be carried flat or horizontally, but always aloft and free.

(d) The flag should never be used as wearing apparel, bedding, or drapery. It should never be festooned, drawn back, nor up, in folds, but always allowed to fall free. Bunting of blue, white, and red, always arranged with the blue above, the white in the middle, and the red below, should be used for covering a speaker's desk, draping the front of the platform, and for decoration in general.

(e) The flag should never be fastened, displayed, used, or stored in such a manner as to permit it to be easily torn, soiled, or damaged in any way.

(f) The flag should never be used as a covering for a ceiling.

(g) The flag should never **have placed upon it, nor on any part of it, nor attached to it any mark, insignia, letter, word, figure, design, picture, or drawing of any nature.**

(h) The flag should never be used as a receptacle for receiving, holding, carrying, or delivering anything.

(i) The flag should never **be used for advertising purposes in any manner whatsoever. It should not be embroidered on such articles as cushions or** handkerchiefs and the like, printed or otherwise impressed on paper napkins or boxes or anything that is designed for temporary use and discard. Advertising signs should not be fastened to a staff or halyard from which the flag is flown.

(j) No part of the flag should ever be used as a costume or athletic uniform. However, a flag patch may be affixed to the uniform of military personnel, firemen, policemen, and members of patriotic organizations. The flag represents a living country and is itself considered a living thing. Therefore, the lapel flag pin being a replica, should be worn on the left lapel near the heart.

(k) The flag when it is in such condition that it is no longer a fitting emblem for display, should be destroyed in a dignified way, preferably by burning.

Note: It is against US Code to stretch the flag across the field during "The Star- Spangled Banner" or be worn on athletes' uniforms. The US Code says this is "Disrespect for the Flag."

NFL fans and owners are angry that black players kneel when the flag is displayed. In fact, on January 30, 2018, President Donald Trump received a standing ovation during his State of the Union address when he voiced his opposition to those who do not stand for the national anthem. But he and others have yet to express their anger to the NFL and others who violate the flag codes while making millions of dollars from its design and symbols and for spreading the flag across the field horizontally so the fans are forced to look down on it, rather than putting it on the flag pole high above the stadium where it belongs, so fans are forced to look up to it. Instead of condemning the black players for kneeling during "The Star-Spangled Banner," the president should have condemned Grammy Award winning Fergie for disgracefully singing the national anthem during the NBA All Star Game (February 18, 2018). Black players merely kneel to stress the importance of what the flag really stands for (justice for all) while others stoop to use the flag for profit. Justice for all is not a given in the NFL; the NFL owners decide what is just.

Racism and Seattle Seahawks' Owner

Long before the Seattle Seahawks played in the Super Bowls of 2005, 2012, and 2013 and fifteen years after the NFL authorized this new franchise, one of its African American front office employees (Lowell Perry Jr.) accused the Seahawks of racial discrimination and threatened to sue and make it public. The Seahawks claimed they had disciplined Perry for not performing his job as instructed. The Seahawks alleged they had complaints from schools and other organizations that the young black employee failed to show up to represent the Seahawks at several events or arrived there late. Angered at the accusations, Seahawk management said the young man (who was the son of a famous NFL player) threatened to call his dad and sue the organization for racial discrimination. The new owners of the team, Ken Behring and Ken Hoffman, instructed general manager Mike McCormack and coach Chuck Knox to resolve the issue as quickly and as quietly as possible (see appendix 6).

A few months earlier, I had interviewed Chuck Knox on a feature story for my newspaper on why NFL teams were reluctant to hire black coaches. During that interview, I learned a lot about Coach Knox and he got to know me. Coach Knox learned that I was well-known in the black community and had a reputation of working with at-risk youth, negotiating truce between rival gangs and working as a fact-finding investigator in racial discrimination lawsuits. It was Coach Knox that recommended Mike McCormack seek my counsel.

McCormack called me and asked if I could negotiate a settlement. I talked with the young man, and he agreed it would be best to leave the organization quietly, provided it gave him a nice severance and a letter of recommendation and commendation. (See appendix 6.) The deal was done and done quietly. Elated that I had saved the organization from public embarrassment, Ken Hoffman (the minority owner) offered me a job as the Seahawk's Community Relations manager. Coach Knox and McCormack were pleased with the offer.

The agreement was set, except for one condition. Mr. Hoffman wanted to meet my family. He invited me to sit with him in their Kingdome suite during the next game. When I arrived, he was shocked that my wife at that time was white. He called me the following Monday to discuss his feelings about inter-racial marriages. He told me that he would get back to me on the job offer. I have been waiting for that phone call for the past twenty-seven years. When Coach Knox and McCormack learned that the owner withdrew his offer, they were furious.

During this same time, the NFL decided to expand the league. The new team was the North Carolina Panthers. McCormack was offered the job of president and because he thought I would be an asset to the new franchise, he asked me to go with him and develop their community relations program. I declined and continued my work with Seattle's inner-city youth, which included working on projects with Harold Reynolds and Ken Griffey Jr. of the Seattle Mariners. Twenty-four years later (2015), I sent the letter in appendix 6 to Ed Goines, the Seahawks general counsel (who happens to be African American) and shared with him the situation of the past and asked if there were any job opportunities that they would consider for my son. He kindly told me they had none. Despite what happened in the past, my sons and I are die-hard Seahawk fans. We have Seahawk T-shirts, sweat shirts, posters, pillows, blankets, cups, calendars and a one of a kind original portrait of the "Legion of Doom" (as a Father's Day present). Some NFL fans and owners would say Hoffman's decision not to hire a person in an inter-racial marriage was "just and fair." As you will see in their Rooney Rule, other NFL owners also found excuses not to hire and interview African Americans.

NFL's Owners and the Rooney Rule

Dan Rooney, the owner of the Pittsburgh Steelers, was one of the first owners to hire a black man as an NFL coach. The wide receiver coach was the father of the young man who had threatened to sue the Seahawks. Lowell Perry Sr.'s coaching career came after he had retired from playing for the Steelers and prior to him obtaining his law degree and becoming co-chairman of the Equal Employment Opportunity Commission. As stated before, Coach Chuck Knox and I had had this discussion regarding black coaches in the NFL during my private interviews with him. Knox was very supportive of having more black coaches in the NFL and criticized the league for not having them.

In 2003, at the urging of Johnnie Cochran (O. J. Simpson's attorney) and other prominent blacks, owner Dan Rooney and NFL commissioner Roger Goodell implemented the Rooney Rule, which mandated that teams must interview at least one minority for positions of general manager or head coach. Before this rule, the NFL had had only six minority assistant coaches in eighty years.

In 2013, a decade after the establishment of the Rooney Rule, coach and sports commentator Tony Dungy stated, "I know the concept is good and something we need to do. Obviously, it's not working the way it should." He was right. In 2018, it was clear that the NFL was not living up to the Rooney Rule when the Raiders offered and hired Jon Gruden as their head coach, paying him one hundred million dollars without interviewing one African American or minority candidate for the job. This is another example of how the NFL and its owners ignore their own policies of equality to satisfy the owner's need. This angered many blacks.

NBA Players Speak Out against Injustice and President's Comments

Not only are NFL players speaking out on injustice, NBA players like Lebron James and Kevin Durant are also speaking out. The two exchanged words with Fox News's Laura Ingram after she said (referring to black athletes): "Must they run their mouths like that?" and "So keep the political commentary to yourself or, as someone once said, shut up and dribble." In other words shut up, stay in your place, and don't be uppity. The exchange took place the week of February 16, 2018, just before the NBA All Star weekend.

As a former guest on the Laura Ingram radio show, I was upset and highly offended by her comments. If anyone has the right to speak out on political issues, it is the professional athlete who pays millions of dollars in state, local, and national taxes and casts his or her vote like any other citizen who may be concerned about the country and the direction it is going.

Prior to the president's offensive name-calling, when he called kneeling athletes—"son(s) of a bitch(es)"—the athletes were relatively quiet and let their kneeling do the talking for them. It is the President, not the athletes, who should be told to keep his comments to himself and just focus on his job of being the president for all people. The president spoke out against the NFL players for kneeling, but he did not speak out when the NFL violated the Rooney Rule by giving Jon Gruden the position of head coach for the Raiders without interviewing one black candidate.

This makes blacks angry.

Chapter 5

King and Kaepernick's Non-Violent Protests versus Protests of White America

Jon Gruden's job offer came on the heels of two years of protests by African American NFL players, led by former 49ers quarterback, Colin Kaepernick. Kaepernick stated that he wanted to bring attention to the injustice of shooting unarmed black men. His protest of kneeling during "The Star-Spangled Banner" angered white fans and some NFL owners. Whites across the country were outraged! To express his anger, President Donald Trump in 2017 sent out a tweet, calling any athlete who protested by kneeling (the protesters were primarily black) a "son of a bitch." Angry white fans and NFL owners claim that sitting down or kneeling during "The Star-Spangled Banner" was disrespectful to the flag and the soldiers who fought and gave their lives for our freedom and the flag.

Kaepernick started the protest by merely silently sitting down in the background. Inspired by his boldness, players from other teams (both black and white), joined Kaepernick; they too took a stand by kneeling. This infuriated Vice President Pence. He attended an NFL game just to walk out when the players knelt. He felt he had a right to be angry and the right to protest by walking out. The black ball players felt they too had the right to be angry and the right to protest to stop *certain* white police officers who violated and disrespected a Constitution that stood for liberty and justice for ALL.

The Right Way to Protest?

Many have complained that kneeling is not the proper way or the positive way to be heard. History shows that America has never approved the way African Americans have protested.

- When Tommie Smith and John Carlos protested at the 1968 Olympics by quietly raising their fists in the air, critics said this non-violent protest was inappropriate.
- When Dr. King protested, he merely marched, and critics condemned him. They said his protests were "disruptive" and his non-violent protests weren't the proper way to bring about change.
- When Rosa Parks sat down to make a stand for equality, they condemned her and said she was "breaking the law."

- When Muhammad Ali protested by choosing to go to jail rather than to fight someone and, as he said, "shoot them for what? They never called me nigger," critics condemned his protest and said he was "un-American—and ungrateful" after making millions in America.
- And when Colin Kaepernick decided to quietly sit down instead of standing during "The Star-Spangled Banner," critics condemned him but offered him and others no acceptable alternatives.

Vice President Pence objected to the NFL players' protests, but he has never objected to America's first protest when colonists felt they weren't being treated fairly. The following is what historians say regarding America's first protest:

Angered with taxation without representation, the "Sons of Liberty" in 1773 dressed up like Native American warriors, went aboard British ships, and threw the tea, which did not belong to them, overboard. They disguised themselves as Native Americans to place the blame on the American Indian. That protest didn't end there; it led to the Revolutionary War, a protest that lasted from 1775 to 1783, where twenty-five thousand were killed in war-related deaths and another twenty-five thousand were wounded, making it the largest and most bloody protest in American history.

As stated before, a black man by the name of Crispus Attucks was to first to die in that protest against British rule. Today we still celebrate this protest, and many claim it was the only way colonists could bring attention to the injustices they suffered at the hands of the British government. In their protest, they used guns to kill those they disagreed with and those who treated them unfairly. Is killing rather than kneeling the kind of protest that NFL owners and fans want African Americans to resort to? The Boston Tea Party and the Revolutionary War are considered the most effective protests in American history, ones that consisted of killing those they disagreed with to get their point across. The patriotic Americans who opposed the NFL players for kneeling have never condemned the participants in the Boston Tea Party and the Revolutionary War for their method of protesting. Killing as a method of protesting didn't stop with the Boston Tea Party. Americans continued to use killing as an effective means of protesting to express their anger for things they did not agree with.

White Protests That Included Killing

The New York Protest of 1863

Angry that President Lincoln instituted a draft to recruit more soldiers for the Union Army during the Civil War, White Irish residents of the city of New York believed their jobs would eventually be taken away by freed blacks (if the Union won the war), so they protested by going on a killing spree, killing as many blacks as possible. Notable historians say they burned down the homes of blacks, burned down businesses and the homes of abolitionists, burned down the Colored Orphanage Asylum, and hung blacks from the lamp posts on the streets of New York. President Lincoln sent troops from Gettysburg to stop the riot, which lasted from July 13 to 16 in 1863. No whites were ever arrested or charged, and no NFL fan or owner has publicly condemned this historical protest.

Detroit Protest of 1863

As in New York, whites who opposed Lincoln's draft attacked blacks in other cities. One historian reported that whites mercilessly beat African Americans and burned down thirty-five buildings in Detroit. Two blacks were killed. No whites were ever arrested or charged, and to our knowledge, no NFL fan or owner has publicly condemned this historical protest.

The 1873 Colfax Protest of Louisiana

On Easter Sunday in 1873 in Colfax, Louisiana, former Confederate soldiers and whites who protested the outcome of the state's gubernatorial election went on a killing rampage, killing a number of blacks. President Ulysses S. Grant sent federal troops to Louisiana to stop the killing. Most historians refer to this event as the Colfax Massacre. No whites were ever arrested or charged, and to our knowledge, no NFL fan or owner has publicly condemned this historical protest.

The 1898 Wilmington Protest Riot

In 1898, several homes and businesses in the black community of Wilmington, North Carolina, were burned to the ground after protesting whites stole the election by threatening to kill any black voters who planned to vote for a black candidate. The killings took place after white protestors drove all the black elected officials from their physical offices. This protest is often referred to as the Wilmington Massacre. Several blacks were shot and killed on the streets of Wilmington. The remaining black women and children found refuge in the nearby swamps. No whites were ever arrested or charged. To our knowledge, no NFL fan or owner has publicly condemned or denounced this historical protest.

Chicago Riot Protest of 1919

Angered that a black young man crossed the line when he swam into an area of the beach that was considered for whites only, whites protested. The protest turned into a Chicago race riot. Thirty-eight people were killed, twenty-three blacks and fifteen whites. It is believed that as a young man, Richard J. Daley, the long-term major of Chicago, participated in the killings of blacks. Mayor Daley never responded when asked if he had participated. No whites were ever arrested or charged, and to our knowledge, no NFL fan or owner has publicly condemned this historical protest.

Tulsa Oklahoma Riot Protest of 1921

White mobs gathered in Tulsa, Oklahoma, when it was reported by the *Tulsa Tribune* that Dick Rowland, a black man, had touched a white woman on an elevator. On the morning of May 30, 1921, the city erupted in a violent protest as thousands of whites took to the street, beating and killing blacks at random. When the dust settled, historians report that three hundred blacks were killed, eight hundred were wounded, over six thousand blacks were arrested, and thirty-five city blocks in the black community were burned to the ground. It was one of the worst and most violent protests in America history. No white was ever arrested or prosecuted, and to our knowledge, no NFL fan or owner has publicly denounced or condemned this historical protest.

1923 Protest Riot in Rosewood, Florida

In Rosewood, Florida, a middle-class black community was burned to the ground and many blacks were killed when whites protested after it was reported that a black man had raped a white girl. After the destruction, they learned that the white young lady had lied. Some historians report that over one hundred blacks were killed during this protest and most of the black businesses and the black church were destroyed. Black churches were always one of first buildings in the black community that white protesters sought to destroy. No whites were ever arrested or charged, and to our knowledge, no NFL fan or owner has publicly condemned this violent historical protest.

I can go on and talk about other protests in Arkansas, Georgia, and Chicago by whites that always resulted in the death of blacks, protests where no whites were ever arrested or charged. Rarely has anyone ever been killed in the "planned" non-violent protests initiated by Rosa Parks, Dr. King, Muhammad Ali, or Colin Kaepernick. The same cannot be said about protests by white Americans. History shows that no black leader publicly called any of the white protestors who killed thousands "sons of bitches."

The Double Standard

When NFL quarterback Cam Newton (a black man) made a comment regarding a female sports reporter asking questions about football plays, sponsors quickly cancelled his endorsement contracts, claiming that his statement was distasteful and disrespected women. But when the public learned that Donald Trump bragged about "grabbing women's pussies," millions of white women and corporate executives lined up to endorse him with their vote to put him in the White House (Trump supporters also included NFL owners who supported his campaign and helped to finance his Inauguration). This is same individual who is now our president and called any black NFL protesters a "son of a bitch" because of the players' method of non-violent protests. Cam Newton apologized for what he said. Donald Trump has yet to offer a sincere apology for what he said and did.

Black men have the right to be angry.

Is Black Anger Justified? | 43

This double standard appears in other areas affecting blacks. Over the years, several thousand African American men have been incarcerated for selling marijuana, and many are still serving time in the same states that have legalized the sale of this drug. However, it is interesting to note that most of those receiving licenses to sell the drug (where states have legalized it) are white.

African Americans do not recommend protesting by killing those who disagree with them or those who treat them unfairly like the participants in the Boston Tea Party and Revolutionary War. Nor do they recommend or support men who make disrespectful sexist comments about women sports reporters or a presidential candidate who brags about "grabbing women's pussies" because he had the power to do so. Blacks do not endorse leaders or anyone else who call another a "son of a bitch" simply because they do not agree with them. It is clear that members of one race can do these things that members of another race cannot.

Black anger is justified.

On Sunday, August 28, 2016, Colin Kaepernick made the following statement during the 49ers NFL media session:

> "People don't realize what's really going on in this country. There are a lot things that are going on that are unjust. People aren't being held accountable. And that's something that needs to change. . . . [T]his country stands for freedom, liberty and justice for all. And it's not happening for all right now."

Kaepernick is right—liberty and justice for all. This is what the flag really stands for and what our black and white soldiers have been fighting for over the past two hundred years, not for racism and injustice. African Americans feel it is racism and injustice that disrespects our soldiers and our flag, not humbly kneeling.

Chapter 6

Employment: Something to Be Angry About

Many Americans feel that after the passage of the 1964 Civil Rights Act, blacks and whites would be on an even playing field, provided that African Americans stayed in school and acquired a good education. Is their assumption true? Yes, in some instances, and no, in others.

Since the beginning of professional sports, most front-office personnel in all three major sports (baseball, basketball, and football) are white (according to the Institute of Diversity and Ethics), even though most of the players on those teams (with the exception of baseball) are black. Most of these players have either a college degree or at least one year of college, and only a few have just a high school education. Many of these black ball players have their own foundations, which focus on education, and others give thousands in scholarships and money for school supplies. If you asked these teams why they have so few blacks in their administrative, front-office support staff, they would provide you with an answer, but not the type of answer that the former Seahawks owner provided for me.

Has education made a difference for blacks? Yes, education has opened many doors; however, some doors remain shut. It is clear that education is not a factor when it comes to front-office jobs in professional sports. Most of their jobs are clerical support or positions that do not require an advanced degree.

For many African Americans, degrees do not guarantee success. According to *Newsweek* magazine, African Americans with graduate degrees in high-paying positions still have their struggles and frustrations. In their November 17, 1993 issue, the magazine featured an eye-opening cover story entitled: "The Hidden Rage of Successful Blacks." The article said: "Though they struggle to hold their anger in check even the most successful blacks find themselves haunted by racial demons."

The ten-page feature provided interviews with several top-level African Americans who shared their race-related frustration. From law partners of large New York law firms to ambassadors of the United States, their stories of disrespect from subordinate white employees to being overlooked and locked out of the "good ole boy clubs" reflected their rage and anger.

From our struggles of not being hired to how we are treated after we are hired are common experiences for many African Americans. I can relate to those mentioned in the *Newsweek* article. One of my first jobs was a Human Resource position with Todd Shipyards. I was the first black hired in an administrative management position in the history of the company. The company's history goes back to old ironclad ships of the *Monitor* and *Merrimack* during the Civil War. Like many other blacks who were the first black hired in management positions, I had to endure racial jokes and name-calling just to put food on my table and pave the way for other African Americans.

There were long periods of unemployment during my career for a variety of reasons, including company downsizing and plant closures during recessions. One year, I wrote in my diary that I had applied for over one thousand jobs only to be told over and over again that I was overqualified. In other situations, I ended up being one of two final candidates for the job (out of five hundred applicants), but was never offered the job. The job consistently went to the white candidate. Oftentimes, my anger turned to tears, but there was nothing I could do but keep applying for work.

One of the brightest times in my job search was when I applied for a Human Resource job at a major law firm. The law firm had several hundred lawyers with offices in Seattle, Chicago, and Washington DC. It represented some of the largest corporations in America, including the Boeing Company. The law firm's employment process included several steps, particularly for this job. The candidate was required to interview not only with senior partners in the law firm but with a panel of employees whom the person would supervise. The panel in this law firm included a support staff primarily consisting of white females. Again, I was one of the final two candidates out of a pool of over five hundred. During the interview, the support staff said I was exactly what they needed in their law firm and that I was far more qualified than the other candidate (who happened to be a white female). They said they were going to recommend that I be offered the job. I was elated. I knew the job was mine.

When I received the call from one of the senior partners to come in, I prepared words to express my appreciation for the job offer. I can remember walking into his plush office. He offered me a seat, but that was all he offered me. He said he called me in to tell me why they weren't offering me the job. He indicated that the staff loved me and I had excellent references, but he thought the other candidate would be better suited for the position because she was a [white] female and that having a female to supervise a predominately [white] female support staff would be best because it would cause fewer potential problems. What he was saying is that he did not want a black man supervising his white female staff. As I walked out of his office, the staff with tears in their eyes thanked me and said they were so sorry. It was difficult holding back my tears as I exited the building. I really needed the job, and my family needed the money. Not only did I have to face my family; also I had to face my white colleagues who were convinced that the only reason blacks were unemployed was because blacks preferred welfare and entitlements rather than a job. I just sat in my car with tears rolling down my cheek. I had to collect myself before going home. So I sat there. It seems like hours. My tears turned to anger and my anger was justified, but there was nothing I could do about it.

* * *

Unlike any other employer in America, professional sports teams rely heavily on their black ball players to fill the stadiums, the living rooms, the dens and sports bars to generate the billion-dollar income that they receive from ticket sales and television contracts. Very few are willing to acknowledge that the income generated by the black ball players pays the salaries of front-office personnel who are primarily white. These facts are often ignored and overlooked by both fans and owners when they talk about race. The reason why most NFL teams have talented black ball players is that they aggressively go after these individuals, but they do not do the same to acquire African American front-office staff. After centuries of systemic employment practices, the median income for African Americans with degrees is still lower than their white counterparts, and the median income of middle class black families is still lower than the income for middle class white families. Consistently, most of the problems African Americans faced in the past and face in the present are systemic.

Chapter 7

Apologies: Lip Service versus Sincerity

African Americans love this country, a country that they helped to build and one that they died for. But like an abused wife brutally raped by her husband and unable to get over the pain when events remind her of that painful past, African Americans continue to see reminders of having been abused—and many continue to experience such abuse. It is a well-known fact that African Americans have been victims of systemic racist practices in every segment of our society. The following acts and pieces of legislation were specifically legislated and designed to target African Americans and no other race.

Systemic Victims in the Field of Medicine

Experiments tested on blacks include the Tuskegee Syphilis Study, a program to see the outcome of six hundred black men infected with syphilis if the syphilis went untreated. The men were told the experiment would only last six months, but instead it lasted forty years (1932-1972). The Centers for Disease Control said by the end of the study in 1972, only 74 of the test subjects were alive. Of the original six hundred men, twenty-eight had died of syphilis, one hundred were dead of related complications, forty of their wives had been infected, and nineteen of their children were born with congenital syphilis.

Another program sterilized teenage black girls in the South without their parents' knowledge or approval (activist Fannie Lou Hamer was a victim). The purpose of the sterilization was to prevent black females from having babies to reduce the number of future black voters. There were other medical studies involving black prisoners, including one where they gave black inmates drugs to study addictions. In all these studies, blacks died, and others never regained their health.

Historians also report that during slavery, "there were separate physicians for slaves and whites because it was believed that slaves' bodies were fundamentally different from whites". Due to this thinking, many slaves became the subjects of physician's experimental interests to help expand both the physician's knowledge and reputation, often resulting in slave's mutilation and death" (WikiVisually).

Systemic Victims in the Field of Education

During slavery, African Americans weren't permitted to read or write. After the passage of the 13th, 14th, and 15th Amendments abolishing slavery, giving blacks citizenship, and the right to vote, many black children were permitted to go to school, but not during the planting and harvest seasons and definitely not with white children. In 1896, the United States Supreme Court sanctioned segregation not only for our schools but also for the rest of our society in *Plessy v. Ferguson*. The government forced blacks to attend inferior segregated schools, and many colleges refused to accept African Americans as medical students. The Department of Education cites one situation when a college was forced to admit a black student. The student was required to sit in the back of the room with a screen in front of him. In 1850, white medical students at Harvard's School of Medicine forced three black students to drop out and leave the campus. The colleges, courts, and legislators systemically victimized blacks in the field of education.

Systemic Victims in the Area of Law

During slavery, legislators passed Fugitive Slave laws and endorsed and recognized individual plantation laws to keep blacks in their place. After the Civil War, legislators passed Jim Crow laws, Black Codes, and a multitude of other laws to regulate the newly freed slaves and keep them in their place. These laws were legislated to specifically target one race and one race only, African Americans.

Court Decisions.

The Dred Scott decision, the Slaughter House case, and *Plessy v. Ferguson* were racially biased verdicts upheld by the US Supreme Court. The appeals to the US Supreme Court were attempts to overturn decisions decided by all-white juries and racist white judges. In 1954, under the leadership of Thurgood Marshall, NAACP attorneys won their first major battle in the US Supreme Court, which was a start to put an end to racist-oriented verdicts. According to the *Oxford Companion to the Supreme Court of the United States*, "Many of the court's decisions were based on the attitudes of the individual justices. By 1837 of the nine justices that sat on the bench, five of them were appointed by Democrats who supported slavery, four others were from slave holding states and only one was considered as anti-slavery." Many condemned the predominately black jury in the O. J. Simpson case, but historically, blacks have consistently had to face all white juries.

Criminal Justice System

Over the years, the courts developed a reputation and a track record of giving black men harsher sentences than their white counter-parts. After the Civil War, black convicts were consistently assigned to work in hazardous prison lease camps providing free labor for rich white businessmen and landowners who were in the business of mining, farming, land development, or building railroads. Historians say these types of prisons were worse than slavery. Blacks were transported from one job site to the next in cages made for wild animal. Many blacks were blown to pieces while working in mines, clearing land and draining swamps.

Systemic Victims in Business

For decades, banks denied blacks bank loans and instead supported improper and unethical business practices to take advantage of uneducated black sharecroppers. The unethical practices often resulted in thousands of black farmers losing their farms. According to the Associated Press, in 1910 African Americans owned over fifteen million acres of farmland in the South, and today they own less than two million acres. In Elaine, Arkansas, historians report that as many as two hundred black farmers were massacred and several others were arrested and executed simply because they met at a black church to discuss how they could stop their white landlords from cheating them out of their cotton crops.

Systemic Victims in Employment

For years, companies and labor unions denied employment opportunities to blacks in a variety of areas simply because of the color of their skin. To counter this, African Americans started their own unions, organizations, and schools to produce skilled craftsmen and academic scholars. These individuals provided services denied, along with training and products that were much needed by their people.

One of African Americans' first trade and academic schools was Booker T. Washington's Tuskegee Institute.

Systemic Victims in the Area of Voting

Whites passed a variety of laws requiring African Americans to pay poll taxes and take ridiculous tests to qualify as voters. Many blacks were killed the night before elections to intimidate them, and others were killed at the voting poll when they attempted to vote. Systemic voting practices targeting blacks remained intact for almost one hundred years and ended (for the most part) with the passage of the Voting Rights Act of 1965.

Systemic Victims in the Area of Politics

Laws were passed to deny African Americans the right to run for office and to register to vote. Efforts to deny African Americans the right to vote and to run for office are well documented in the chronicles of history. In 1868, twenty-seven duly-elected black Republican legislators were driven from office in the General Assembly of the state of Georgia, despite the fact that Republicans then held both the governorship and a majority in the state senate. That action, along with the subsequent Camilla Massacre, which left about a dozen black protestors dead and thirty wounded, led the US Congress to reimpose military rule to the state and to ban Georgia's newly elected congressmen from taking their seats in the next House of Representatives. There were similar incidents in Wilmington, North Carolina, in 1898 and in Colfax, Louisiana, in 1873.

Gerrymandering

Gerrymandering was a court and legislative-approved process of redistricting to diminish and dilute the power of the black vote in various legislative districts throughout the country. Historians report that in 1912, Congress introduced the greatest number of laws in the history of our country to support segregation policies.

Systemic Victims in the Military

The United States government forced African Americans to serve in a segregated military. From the Civil War to the integration of the military under President Truman, even though blacks served gallantly and courageously, they received less benefits and opportunities than their white counterparts. The military rejected (baseball great) Jackie Robinson's first application to attend Military Officer Training School and later attempted to court martial him because Jackie refused to sit in the back of a military bus. Joe Louis supported Jackie throughout his entire ordeal by writing to the War Department and threatened to no longer do exhibition fights for the military.

Systemic Victims in Housing

Courts permitted homeowner associations and neighborhood organizations to deny African Americans the right to live in what were called white neighborhoods. Through court approved redlining, realtors were able to devalue properties in areas where African Americans were the primary residents. It remained this way for 346 years (until 1965) when legislation creating the US Department of Housing and Urban Development (HUD) was passed. The stated purpose of HUD is "to create strong, sustainable, inclusive communities and quality affordable homes for all. HUD is working to strengthen the housing market to bolster the economy and protect consumers; meet the need for quality affordable rental homes; utilize housing as a platform for improving quality of life; build inclusive and sustainable communities free from discrimination."

Systemic Victims in Sports
Major League Baseball

For years, Major League Baseball (MLB) denied blacks the opportunity to play in what they called the major leagues. Even though Jackie Robinson, Willie Mays, and Hank Aaron were eventually given the green light to play, they (and their families) were called "nigger" and faced death threats from angry white fans. Hotels in certain cities refused to let them stay with their white teammates, and restaurants refused to serve them. There were times when white teams refused to take the field to avoid "playing with those niggers."

National Basketball Association

The NBA did very little to support black players like Bill Russell and K. C. Jones when they were faced with racism by other teams, and like black MLB players, they were often denied the right to sleep in the same hotels as their teammates.

National Football League

It took decades before the NFL was willing to give blacks the opportunity to play quarterbacks and to be seriously considered for positions as head coaches and general managers.

There were systemic racist practices in the field of entertainment. Entertainers such Lena Horne, Nat King Cole, Louie Armstrong, and Sammy Davis Jr. could not stay in the same hotels where they were headliners. In entering the hotel, they were required to enter through the kitchens. The so-called "Chitlin Circuit" (black nightclubs and other venues) were established to give black entertainers a place to perform. When Dick Clark's *American Bandstand* barred blacks from dancing on the show, blacks started their own show, *Soul Train*, as an alternative. White Americans as a race have never had these same types of racial barriers, operating simultaneously (sometimes for hundreds of years) to restrict and to deny members of their race their constitutional rights simply because of the color of their skin.

Despite decades and in some cases centuries of systemic racist practices specifically designed to target African Americans, only a handful of organizations that were responsible for these injustices have offered sincere formal apologies and/or attempted to compensate African Americans for these injustices.

One may say, "What's problem? These barriers no longer exist for blacks." The question is: Were these barriers removed because of remorse, or were they removed because America finally realized that blacks were a $500 billion-dollar-plus consumer market? Everything that happened to African Americans (pro or con) could not have happened without the sanction of those who controlled America, whites.

In 2005, the United States Senate passed Resolution 39, a resolution "apologizing to the victims of lynching and the descendant of those victims for the failure of the Senate to enact ant-lynching legislation."

In 2008, the House of Representatives of the United States passed Resolution 194 apologizing to African Americans for slavery and the era of Jim Crow.

In 2009, the United States Senate issued an apology for the "fundamental injustice, cruelty, brutality and inhumanity of slavery of African American" (see appendix 8).

Despite the various forms of apologies from government officials, none has included reparations and compensation that other groups were blessed to receive. Native Americans received portions of the land they lost during the war. Interned Japanese Americans received reparations after the war for their losses. The country of Japan received eighteen billion dollars (in today's value) to rebuild after America bombed Japan, and under the Marshall Plan, America gave Europe what is equivalent $182 billion to rebuild its war-torn communities after Germany's bombing, but America has yet to give African Americans one penny for their free labor in building America and making it one of the richest countries in the world.

The billions given to other nations and groups include money African American employees paid in federal income taxes. So we ask: Were the government's apologies sincere? Usually when one apologizes, the person finds some way to make up the malignancy or replace what was taken (as the United States did with Japan). The US government and its representatives never attempted to pay African Americans for the destructive policies that affected the entire race or for the hundreds of years of free labor. Unlike Japan, African Americans never bombed America—they only built America, including rebuilding the White House after it was burned down in the War of 1812.

Let me summarize. After three hundred years of slavery, African Americans volunteered for the military. They were sent to Europe and gallantly fought and gave their lives to save Europe. After World War II ended, they came home to deteriorating ghettos (communities) while America sent Europe $182 billion to rebuild their communities. Included in that $182 billion were taxes paid by African Americans workers. Then sixty-four years later (2009), Congress gave African Americans a piece of paper to apologize for slavery. Europe got $182 billion, and blacks got ghettos and the pieces of papers in Appendix 8.

This makes blacks angry.

The following is from President Lincoln's inaugural address on March 4, 1865, with his comments regarding those who profited from slavery:

> The Almighty has His own purposes. . . . Yet, if God wills that it [the war] continue until all the wealth piled up by the bondsman's two hundred and fifty years of unrequited toil be sunk, and until every drop of blood drawn with the lash shall be paid by another drawn with the sword, as was said three thousand years ago, so still it must be said "the judgements of the Lord are true and righteous altogether."

Apology versus Reality

Many say we have come a long ways. Perhaps we have but:

1. Most whites today do not have a close friend who is black.

2. Most blacks today do not have a close friend who is white.

3. Most blacks still go to predominately black churches.

4. Most whites still attend predominately white churches.

5. Most whites live in the suburbs or rural areas and have very little to do with blacks.

6. Most blacks live in the inner-city and have very little to do with whites.

7. Most white pastors are not friends with local black pastors.

8. Most black pastors are not friends with local white pastors.

9. The vast majority of Americans have never had a person of another race over for dinner.

10. Most whites have never initiated or led discussions on racism.

11. The unemployment rate for blacks has been consistently higher than that for whites.

12. The median income for black families has been consistently lower than that for white families.

As indicated in the previous chapter, "Employment: Something to Be Angry About," it appears that blacks have been merely tolerated and not really accepted.

Chapter 8

Taking Responsibility for Ourselves

Tired of the injustice and the shooting of unarmed black young men, on July 13, 2016, during the ESPY Awards, Carmelo Anthony, Chris Paul, Dwayne Wade, and Lebron James stood before a packed audience and denounced the injustice and challenged African Americans to go back to their communities and make positive changes (see appendix 7).

One hundred twenty years earlier in 1896, Booker T. Washington also had a packed audience at one of his Negro Conferences, and this is what he said:

> The aim will be, as in the four previous years, to bring together for a quiet conference, not politicians, but the representatives of the common, hardworking farmers and mechanics and the back bone and sinew of the Negro race, the ministers and teachers. I want to emphasize the object of these conferences. When they were first instituted, it was to confine ourselves mainly to the conditions within our own power to remedy. We might discuss many wrongs which should be righted; but it seems to me that it is best to lay hold of the things we can put right rather than those we can do nothing but find fault with. To be perfectly frank with each other; state things as they are; do not say anything for mere sound, or because you think it will please one or displease another; let us hear the truth on all matters. We have many things to discourage and disappoint us, and we sometimes feel that we are slipping backwards; but I believe, if we do our duty in getting property, Christian education, and character, in some way or other the sky will clear up, and we shall make our way onward.

One hundred six years later (1992), columnist William Raspberry of the *Washington Post* expressed similar feelings during an interview with *Newsweek* magazine. On April 6, 1992, *Newsweek* reported that Raspberry said, "Black Americans are still captives of the 60's and its political goals. Racism and poverty are not the reasons why we are in the situation we are in today. To try to link our solutions to elective politics is to put government on the hook for things we should do ourselves."

Far too many people are waiting for the government or a particular political party to do what we can do ourselves. This is not to say that, as voters and taxpayers, we do not have the right to demand certain things from our government and our political representatives. We do have this right, and we should exercise this right. After all, it is we, the taxpayers that employ these individuals to work for us. With our tax dollars, we provide both their salaries and the physical office space that they occupy (for both the Democrats and the Republicans).

African Americans should never be too embarrassed to ask for government funding (our tax dollars) to develop self-help programs for our people. Contrary to what many are led to believe, major corporations, not our nation's welfare recipients, are the biggest recipients and benefactors of our tax dollars. We often overlook the fact that our government purchases tanks, planes, desks, chairs, computers, copiers, and millions of other items from the private sector, (i.e., corporations). Each day, these corporations compete for our tax dollars through their powerful lobbyists. In 1968, there were only sixty-two registered lobbyists in Washington, DC; in 2018, there are approximately ten thousand, all lobbying for our tax dollars to fund corporate programs and projects. If corporate America isn't embarrassed or afraid to ask for our tax dollars to benefit itself and its stockholders, as African American taxpayers, we shouldn't be embarrassed to make those same requests on behalf of our people. Any money coming from the government is merely a rebate of what we have already given them. Without our taxes, the government has no money to give.

Requests for government funding should be made, regardless of which political party is in power. Dr. King held both parties accountable, and we should do the same. Dr. King was invited to the White House during President Eisenhower's administration, and he was invited to the White House during the Kennedy/Johnson administration. He played a major role in bringing about social change and major Civil Rights legislation because he was willing to work with both parties.

We not only have the responsibility to hold both parties accountable; we also must be willing to do what our people did in the past.

They trusted in God and their God-given gifts and talents and then used their faith and talents to make a difference. We cannot stand around expecting others to do what we can do for ourselves.

In the afterword of Dr. Kings' book, *Why We Can't Wait*, Rev. Jesse Jackson said:

> Had Dr. King waited for an elected official or a politician to be bold enough to do the right thing and change the law to include every American in the American Dream, change would have never come. Dr. King knew that the key to unlocking American Apartheid was not in the White House or any governor's mansion. It was in the homes of average citizens. Dr. King knew that if the people stood up and used their collective power, they could change an entire nation. So home by home, congregation by congregation, city by city, Dr. King convinced the people that they had the power if only they would use it.

Another writer put it this way:

> There was an important job to be done and Everybody was sure that Somebody would do it. Anybody could have done it, but Nobody did it. Somebody got angry about that, because it was Everybody's job. Everybody thought Anybody could do it, but Nobody realized that Everybody wouldn't do it. It ended up that Everybody blamed Somebody when Nobody did what Anybody could have done.

Both Jesse Jackson and Al Sharpton would probably agree that they are not the ones who are really making a difference in our communities; it is the millions of *Nobodies*, *Anybodies*, and *Everybodies* (selfless volunteers) who volunteer their time to support a variety of community- based social programs. Those programs include coaching, economic development, tutoring and mentoring inner-city youth, as well as preparing both youth and adults for college, the trades, new careers, and better-paying jobs.

African Americans do not need leaders who will merely use their lips to lecture in the legislature. They need leaders who will lend a helping hand to change their community. As Lebron James advocated, every black leader, politician, professional athlete, and entertainer should return to his or her community once a year, put on work clothes, and physically do something to improve the community like Doug Baldwin of the Seattle Seahawks. Doug is building a community center in a low-income neighborhood in Renton, Washington. We all should get involved in projects that include cleaning up neighborhoods, building teen centers, tutoring, serving the needy, painting and remodeling recreational facilities, schools, senior citizens' homes, and assisting single parents with their children and teachers with their classes. We must always remember that beautiful, peaceful communities are not legislated into existence. These types of communities are built and developed by the dedicated members of the community.

The History of Blacks Helping Blacks

If our modern-day African American community had what our predecessors had, i.e.,

perseverance with a tremendous determination to succeed,
unity in the community,
a love for their people,
and a strong faith in God;

and if our predecessors had what we currently have, i.e.,
a multitude of black millionaires and billionaires and
a Jim Crow–free society based on laws that guaranteed their rights as citizens;

then today's generation of African Americans would be one of the most powerful and one of the most revered groups in the entire world.

Unlike many successful blacks today, who give children backpacks for back-to-school or turkeys to families during the holiday seasons, during the era of slavery and Jim Crow, blacks were committed to helping members of their own race, even if it meant losing their lives, their fortunes, and/or their careers. History records that many freed blacks risked their lives to rescue members of their race.

The following are just a few of the many unsung heroes of the past who unified and dedicated their lives to meet the needs of their own people and, in so doing, provided broad shoulders for future generations to stand on.

John Mason, a relatively unknown free slave, traveled to the South numerous times to free a total of thirteen hundred slaves through the Underground Railroad network, according to Wilbur H. Siebert in *The Underground Railroad from Slavery to Freedom: A Comprehensive History*, first published in 1898 (see appendix 10). John Mason did so even though there was a reward for his capture. During his last rescue attempt, he was caught, severely punished, and remained a slave for the rest of his life. While Harriet Tubman and several other blacks unified and risked their lives to free their black brothers and sisters, other freed blacks worked several years to save enough money to buy the freedom of others.

Frederick Douglass was a freed slave. When the Civil War broke out, he was free but not satisfied. Not satisfied because millions of his black brothers and sisters were still in bondage. Instead of enjoying the fruits of freedom, Douglass was preoccupied with gaining freedom for his people. During a meeting with President Abraham Lincoln, he convinced Lincoln that other free blacks like himself were willing to fight and even face death just to free their people. Lincoln was shocked when over 180,000 free black men voluntarily enlisted in the Union Army and pledged to give their lives to save their people.

Elizabeth Keckley was one of the wealthiest black women in America during the Civil War. As a dress designer for wealthy women (like Mary Todd Lincoln and the wife of Jefferson Davis), she earned enough money to buy her freedom and eventually hired twenty employees to work for her. Even though she was very wealthy and worked with the elites of that society, she never forgot her people. In 1862, Miss Keckley co-founded the Contraband Relief Association, an organization of African American women who provided social services for freed slaves in the Washington, DC, area. She would also take Mrs. Lincoln down to the Soldier's Home where they would care for wounded soldiers. Miss Keckley never forgot where she came from and never forgot her people. Being a personal friend of the Lincolns, she often advised President Lincoln on matters pertaining to African Americans.

Booker T. Washington started Tuskegee Institute with only one goal in mind, providing African Americans with the necessary skills to improve their lives and to enable them to start businesses of their own. The primary goal of most black educators during that time was to give black children a quality education. In the late 1800s, with limited finances and meager salaries, educators like Booker T. and Mary McLeod Bethune, along with hundreds of other committed black teachers, started and taught in their own schools. Their commitment to black education went far beyond providing backpacks for black children. Their goal was to produce outstanding young men and women of character.

Dr. George Washington Carver had several offers to teach at other institutions but chose instead to accept an invitation from Booker T. Washington to teach at Tuskegee Institute. Dr. Carver, like Booker T., was committed to helping the poor black farmer. Booker and Carver never forgot their people and never forgot where they came from. Biographers report that Carver turned down a salary in excess of one hundred thousand dollars to work for Henry Ford in the early 1900s. He continued his work at Tuskegee and did so for the rest of his life because he felt that his people needed him. Dr. George Washington Carver was buried next to Booker T. Washington on the campus of Tuskegee. His epitaph reads: " He could have added fortune to his fame, but caring for neither, he found happiness and honor in being helpful to the world."

Dr. Daniel Hale Williams was troubled after successfully performing one of the first open heart surgeries in 1893 because black doctors and nurses were denied access to hospitals to complete their internship. To meet this need, in 1891, this prominent black doctor started Provident Hospital in Chicago (the first black hospital in America), along with a nursing school for young African American women. In 1895, he co-founded the National Medical Association for black doctors. Today this organization represents the interest of more than thirty thousand African American physicians and the patients they serve with nearly 129 affiliated societies throughout the nation and US territories. The organization was formed simply because black doctors were committed to providing healthcare for their people.

John Merrick was a former slave who worked very hard and became a very wealthy businessman owning several businesses, including a chain of barbershops and an enormous amount of real estate. Because white insurance companies refused to insure blacks, he started the North Carolina Mutual Insurance Company (in 1898) to provide life insurance for his people. North Carolina Mutual Insurance Company became the largest black insurance company in America, insuring thousands of African Americans.

R. D. Evans, an attorney, tried a case in Waco, Texas, in 1919 to prevent the Democratic Party from forbidding "colored people" to vote in the primaries. Shortly after, in 1925, Evans and a few other black attorneys founded the National Bar Association (NBA). Their new organization was committed to providing legal assistance for poor blacks. Today the National Bar Association is the nation's oldest and largest national network of predominantly African-American attorneys and judges. It represents the interests of approximately sixty thousand lawyers, judges, law professors, and law students. The NBA is organized around twenty-three substantive law sections, nine divisions, twelve regions, and eighty affiliate chapters throughout the United States and around the world. The NBA was specifically started by a group of black attorneys to provide quality legal services for their people.

Negro Baseball League Prior to the formation of the Negro Baseball League, inspirational gospel music in the black church was the primary entertainment for the black community. After the formation of the Negro leagues in the mid 1800's, Negro baseball became one of the most sought-after entertainments for black families. Blacks unified and formed their own leagues and like the black church (for the most part), it was an institution solely owned and controlled by blacks. From the mid-1800s to the mid-1900s, there were over two hundred all-black baseball teams in America and Negro baseball became the number one live entertainment in black communities throughout the country.

Appreciating Those Who Paved the Way for Us

In writing a script for a new movie on the Negro Baseball League, I had the privilege of interviewing the late great Buck O'Neil (a former player of the Negro Baseball League). I asked: "How many of the current black major league players have supported and visited the beautiful multi-million dollar Negro Baseball Museum [which he founded] in Kansas City?" With tears in his eyes, the old man dropped his head and said, "Very few."

Each season, a number of black millionaire baseball players take the field without giving one thought about Jackie Robinson, the Willie Mays, Hank Aarons, and other black baseball athletes who paved the way for their success. This may also be true for black professional athletes in other sports, as well as for blacks in other professions.

From the pa–stors of our mega churches to professional black athletes and entertainers, far too many successful African Americans seem to be preoccupied with living for the moment rather than realizing the need to recognize and honor those who gave their all and paved the way for their success. Very few seem as committed as their predecessors who unified to meet the pressing needs of their own people.

I often ask:

Do the Denzel Washingtons and the Hallie Berrys ever think about the Louie Armstrongs, the Lena Horns, and the Nat King Coles who paved the way for their success? Individuals who were forced to exit the Las Vegas casinos (through the kitchens after their performances) and forced to travel to the ghetto on the west side to stay in run-down hotels and boarding houses, simply because they were black?

Do our black doctors and dentists ever think about the first black medical students who paved the way for their success? Individuals who were expelled from Harvard's School of Medicine simply because they were black and others who were forced to sit in the back of the class behind screens that separated them from other students as a condition to attend those medical schools?

Do our hip-hop and pop artists ever think about the Motown artists who paved the way for their success? Individuals who traveled by bus and were forced to play and stay in inferior segregated facilities?

Do our professional black athletes ever think about those who paved the way for their success? Individuals like Jesse Owens, Jackie Robinson, Joe Louis, Bill Russell, and Arthur Ashe, black athletes who made very little money (compared to those today) but endured racism to secure a place for future black and Latino athletes?

Do our black educators ever think about those who paved the way for their success? Individuals who taught in the poorly equipped sub-standard one-room schoolhouses with second-hand outdated books and materials?

Do our black preachers from mega churches ever think about their predecessors? Country black preachers who were forced to walk to church (if they did not own a horse or a buggy) to preach to a congregation that could barely read or write, congregations that were made up of members who oftentimes had no money so they compensated their pastors with meat from their farms and vegetables from their gardens, black pastors who laid the foundation for future black churches?

Those mentioned above represent the foundation of today's successful African Americans. No building, no matter how beautiful, will ever be more important than the less attractive foundation on which it stands.

In the past, African Americans knew that they needed each other. They also knew that unity in the community was a must for their survival. Unity was emphasized throughout their society. In a speech by Frederick Douglass in 1883, he told the National Convention of Colored Men the following:

> If the six millions of colored people of this country, armed with the Constitution of the United States, with a million votes of their own to lean upon, and millions of white men at their back, whose hearts are responsive to the claims of humanity, have not sufficient spirit and wisdom to organize and combine to defend themselves from outrage, discrimination and oppression, it will be idle for them to expect that the Republican party or any other political party will organize and combine for them or care what becomes

of them. Men may combine to prevent cruelty to animals, for they are dumb and cannot speak for themselves; but we are men and must speak for ourselves, or we shall not be spoken for at all. . . .

. . . Parties were made for men, not men for parties.

Final Thoughts

Again, as black men, we are more than justified to be angry, but we must channel that anger and transform the negative energies into positive constructive projects to rebuild our communities. It won't be easy, but nothing that is worthwhile comes easy. As a child, my mother often read me stories from the Pittsburgh Courier newspaper, it was the largest black newspaper in America at that time. The following poem is one that she read to me from the Courier's January 14, 1956 edition—written by William Henry Huff. I often read his poem:

> Your knocking me is boosting me
> You're kicking me upstairs
> But this you do not seem to see
> It's helping my affairs.
> You see I'm like a rubber ball
> Each knock sends me up higher;
> No knock will ever make me fall
> Or whine or be a crier.

Harriet Beecher Stowe

Chapter 9

Embracing Our White Allies

In November of 2017 a group of African American NFL Players met with NFL owners in New York to talk about race and social issues. The NFL proposed to contribute nearly $100 million to causes considered important to African American communities. Some players were skeptical and questioned whether there would be any strings attached like forcing them to abandon their Constitutional rights of Freedom of Speech to protest. At the time of this publication, those issues are still being negotiated. It is important that African Americans know their enemies and know their allies.

Throughout history, African Americans have always had a remnant number of white allies. In 1835 over 435,000 whites were members of various anti-slavery societies. Thousands made up the Underground Railroad (see Appendix 9). Over 400,000 whites fought in the Civil War (many with the intent to free the black slave). Inspired by their faith White Christians felt that it was their God-given duty and responsibility to stand with their black brothers. African American men must not become bitter because of racial injustice nor should we ever alienate our white allies. Instead we must channel our anger and use it for good and recognize and embrace those whites who are sincere allies. We know about the problems in the past, but what is not commonly known are those whites who gave their lives and risked everything they had for our freedom and Civil Rights (see Appendix 10). The following is a brief review of the role allied whites played in our historical past. History called these dedicated Christians, "Abolitionist" (not all Abolitionist were Christians, but most were). (See the list of the names of those involved in the Underground Railroad in Appendix 9).

Speaking of the Abolitionist Movement, Princeton's History Professor, James McPherson said, "*Most historians have paid little attention to the abolitionist movement after 1860.... Early in the war, abolitionists outlined a broad program of emancipation, employment of Negro soldiers in the Union Army, creation of a Freedman Bureau, government assistance for the education of the freedmen, civil and political equality for all black men, and grants of confiscated land to the freed slaves. Under military pressures of war and the political pressures of the reconstruction, the Republican Party adopted all of these policies....*"[1]

---

1 The Struggle of Equality pp. xi Preface

Many historians are now acknowledging that a great number of the Abolitionists were inspired by their Christian faith, and many gave their lives for the cause. When placed on trial for his raid on the federal arsenal at Harper's Ferry, Virginia, (in 1859), Abolitionist, John Brown, said these words just before his execution. *"Had I interfered in the manner on behalf of the rich, the powerful and the intelligent, every man in this court would have deemed it an act worthy of reward. But I interfered on behalf of God's despised poor. I did no wrong, but right."*

In one of his final letters Brown wrote: *"I commend you all to Him whose mercy endureth forever, to the God of my father whose I am and whom I serve. He will never leave you nor forsake you. Finally, my dearly beloved, be of good comfort. Be sure to remember and follow my advice, and my example too, so far as it has been consistent with the holy religion of Jesus Christ, in which I remain a most firm and humble believer. Never forget the poor, nor think anything in them to be lost in you, even though they may be black as Ebedmelech, the Ethiopian eunuch, who cared for Jeremiah in the pit of the dungeon; or as black as the one to whom Philip preached Christ. Here, before God, in the presence of these witnesses, I consecrate my life to the destruction of Slavery."*[2]

Under the Fugitive Slave Laws, Abolitionists and their children were harassed, beaten and many were even murdered for assisting runaways slaves. The law also permitted the confiscation of land, homes and other property to discourage participation in the Underground Railroad, but it did not discourage individuals like Levi Coffin, a (white) Quaker who was considered to be the president of the Underground Railroad. To discourage Arthur Tappan, a wealthy white retailer from New York, they burned his home, cancelled his bank loans, cancelled his insurance policy on his business, and cancelled shipments on the products he ordered. When they offered to reinstate all that was taken from him if he would resign from the New York Anti-slavery Society, he responded, *"I'll hang first."*

By 1832, over 400,000 persons were members of the various Anti-Slavery Societies, and they were committed to doing everything within their power to assist the run-away slaves. Hannah Gibbons hid slaves on her small farm because she said the Bible told her *"to love her neighbors."*

---

2 America's God and Country Encyclopedia of Quotations page 77

Attorney Isaac Tatum Hopper successfully defended hundreds of runaway slaves in the northern courts of law. John Rankin and his seven sons were attacked by pro-Slavery mobs over 100 times for their participation in the Underground Railroad.

Dr. Alexander Ross, (a rich, prominent and renown northern doctor) infiltrated the South during his lecture tours, only to arm slaves with guns, food and compasses to aid in their escape from the plantations.

In 1775, Abolitionist (and former Slave Trader) John Newton, was sent word from the University of New Jersey that the school made him an honorary Doctor of Divinity. He turned down the honor and stated that because of his involvement in the slave trade, he would *"never accept any diploma, except it came from poor Blacks."* One day, with a repentant heart he sat down and wrote these words:

"Amazing grace how sweet the sound.
That saved a wretch like me.
I once was lost, but now I'm found,
Was blind but now I see."

These individuals represent thousands of unsung heroes who were inspired by their faith to fight against those who wanted to expand their slave trade business into the new northern states. The Abolitionist Movement was perhaps one of the most successful faith-based programs in American history. This is not to say that all abolitionists were Christians, but a vast majority of them were, including Susan B. Anthony, a Quaker, who was inspired by her abolitionist father.

While Susan devoted much of her time and attention to fighting for women's rights, children of other abolitionists continued their parent's work by providing education and new legislation for the newly freed slaves. Several of these individuals worked with the American Missionary Association (AMA), a faith-based organization dedicated to opening new schools in the south to educate the American Negro. Professor James McPherson reports that when the AMA sent white teachers to southern communities to educate Negroes, the old time southern hospitality was immediately transformed into southern hostility.

Professor McPherson said: "*Southern hostility to Yankee teachers sometimes went beyond ostracism and verbal abuse. In times of political excitement during Reconstruction many missionaries were threatened, beaten, and murdered. The AMA reported several incidents similar to the one in which a group of masked men took a teacher from his house in North Carolina in 1874, tied him up, and after threatening to kill him if he did not leave the state gave him 100 lashes with a bullwhip. The founder and president for nearly 30 years of Shaw University, Henry Tupper of Massachusetts, was often harassed by the Ku Klux Klan and once hid all night in a cornfield with his wife and two children to avoid an assassination attempt.*

In 1871, a college treasurer went to a nearby town on business, had dinner with a Black family, and after leaving a prayer meeting at a Negro church was ambushed by five men who fired at him seven times and left him for dead. The shots had missed, however, the treasurer returned to his hotel, where at 3:00 AM 30 masked men dragged him from his bed, took him to the woods, and gave him 61 lashes with a hickory whip.

The 1874 elections were a particularly tense time; as one teacher put it, to be for weeks in a constant expectation of being murdered or burned out, and without losing faith in God, is something of a strain on the nerves.

In 1879, the Northern Methodists compiled a list of 34 attacks on their missionaries and teachers in the past decade; 19 of the victims were White and 15 Black, three of the whites and four of the Blacks were killed.

The AMA tried for several years to cooperate with local [southern] *school boards. So long as* Republicans *were in power this arrangement worked out reasonably well. But when the* Democrats *began to regain control of the South the dual support foundered and eventually collapsed. In Memphis the* Democrats *dismissed all AMA teachers, forcing the association to withdraw from the jointly sponsored Lincoln School and found LeMoyne Institute in its place. In Columbus, Mississippi,* Democrats *drove out the Union Academy's northern teachers with threats of violence and then closed the school in 1871.*"[3]

---

3 pp.174-175 The Abolitionist Legacy: From Reconstruction to the NAACP

Abolitionist Influence On NAACP & Negro Colleges

Throughout history, African Americans have had a remnant number of white allies. In 1835 over 435,000 whites were members of various anti-slavery societies. Thousands made up the Underground Railroad. And over 400,000 fought in the Civil War (many with the intent) to free the black slave. Inspired by their faith White Christians felt that it was their God-given duty and responsibility to stand with their black brothers. African American men must not be bitter because of the past. Instead they must channel their anger for good and recognize and embrace those whites who are sincere allies. We know about the problems in the past, but what are not commonly known are those whites who gave their lives for our freedom and Civil Rights. The following is a brief review of the role they played in our historical past. History called these dedicated Christians, "Abolitionist". (Also see the 8 page list of the names of those involved in the Underground Railroad in Appendix 4)..

While the violence discouraged some, others were more determined. The determined ones included John D. Rockefeller and Oswald Garrison Villard. Many of us may have heard of billionaire John D. Rockefeller and possibly even Oswald Garrison Villard, but few have heard about their work on behalf of blacks particularly in the areas of social justice and education. Oswald Garrison Villard, and Mary White Ovington who came from a long line of abolitionists, were the original founders and directors of the NAACP, and John D. Rockefeller was the Republican philanthropist who donated millions of dollars to black colleges.

In reference to Villard and Ovington's work, historian John Hope Franklin said, *"In 1909, liberal whites such as Mary White Ovington, Oswald Garrison Villard, and William English Walling issued a call for a conference to consider the plight of African Americans.* In that same year, these key individuals met and formed what is now known as the NAACP or the National Association for the Advancement of Colored People. In confirming Professor Franklin's findings, the Negro Almanac reports, that the formation of the *"NAACP was largely the brainchild of Ovington, Villard and Walling, three white individuals"*[4] (The Negro Almanac Fifth Edition page 260).

---

4 The Negro Almanac Fifth Edition page 260

By 1936, these individuals and other white liberals continued to play a major role in the NAACP, focusing primarily on eliminating the lynching of black citizens. According to Juan Williams, author of Thurgood Marshall: American Revolutionary: *"as the organization grew, it depended heavily on white philanthropists for its financial support."*

Although the work of Ovington, Villard and Walling was very significant, they, and other (well deserving) white Republicans are often overlooked in the chronicles of Black History. Such is the case with Henry L. Morehouse, and Laura Spelman, two white individuals who worked very hard to establish and maintain some of our historical black colleges.

Laura Spelman's work with black schools and colleges had a profound influence on both her husband and her son, John D. Rockefeller and John D. Rockefeller Jr. In 1902, father and son set up a General Education Board to assist southern black schools. By the end of the first decade the board had donated over $33,000,000 toward furthering the goals of black education. By 1921, they had donated another $96,000,000, black schools and colleges were the recipients of some of this money as well. Spelman College for African American women bears the name of this devout Christian woman (who was also the daughter of an abolitionist father).

Henry L. Morehouse was the Executive Secretary of the Home Mission Society, an organization that financed and started many of the first black schools and colleges. Morehouse received national recognition when a prominent black college in Atlanta Georgia (Augusta Institute) decided to honor him by naming their school after him (Morehouse College). All of these individuals were either devout Abolitionists or Radical Republicans who were dedicated to helping blacks achieve equality through quality education. Many prominent African Americans leaders were the benefactors of these faith-based schools and the funding provided by Christian and Republican philanthropists. Dr. Martin Luther King graduated from Morehouse College and it is reported that the Rev. Jesse Jackson received a scholarship from the Rockefeller Fund to attend Chicago Theological Seminary.

During Reconstruction, educating the newly freed slaves was also a high priority for other faith-based groups and missionary societies. Again, McPherson tells us, *"Baptist freedmen's schools were sustained at first mainly by New England abolitionists in the denomination. When Henry L. Morehouse became secretary of the Home Mission Society in 1879, he made black education the society's main work. Morehouse served as executive secretary from 1879 to 1893, field secretary from 1893-1902, and executive secretary again from 1902 until his death in 1917. Thomas Morgan was executive secretary from 1893 to 1902. Both men came to maturity as abolitionist in the turbulent 1850's; Morgan commanded four regiments of black troops in the war.*

By 1870 most of the Quaker societies were supporting 47 elementary and six secondary schools. Many of the first and second generation abolitionist who went south as founders, presidents, principals, and teachers of freedmen's schools spent the rest of their lives in this work.

The two presidents who built **Howard University** *from a struggling institution to the foremost black university in the country were lifelong abolitionists: William W. Patton was president from 1877 to1889, and died in office; Jeremiah E. Rankin served from 1890 to 1903, dying a year after his retirement. Wilbur P. Thirkield was president of Howard from 1906 to 1912.*

Atlanta University's *founder and first president (1867-1885) was Edmund Asa Ware, who had been converted to abolitionism as a young man by reading Uncle Tom's Cabin. The founder of* **Fisk University** *was Erastus M. Cravath. Cravath had been brought up by an Abolitionist father and had attended two integrated colleges (New York Central College and Oberlin). He had been American Missionary Association's district and field secretary for 10 years before assuming the presidency of Fisk.*

Abolitionists who headed Methodist schools included George Whipple Hubbard of **Meharry Medical College.** *Joseph Robert, a southerner who left his native section in 1850 because he hated slavery, became the first president of* **Morehouse College,** *which was an institution that had three name changes and one location change.*

In 1915 the editor of the Negro Year Book estimated that over the past half century northern sources had contributed **$57 million** *to Negro education and blacks themselves had provided an additional* **$24 million.**"[5]

---

5 The Abolitionist Legacy From Reconstruction to the NAACP pp.154-159

Black Colleges

The following is a list of a few of the Black schools and colleges started by various Missionary Societies of the North. Again, these schools were financed, funded and sponsored by prominent Republicans and their Abolitionist supporters, while the Democrats with brutal force opposed every effort that two groups put forth to educate the American Negro.

School	Date	Place
Morehouse College	1867	Atlanta, GA
Howard University	1867	Washington D.C.
Spelman Seminary	1881	Atlanta, GA
Shaw University	1865	Raleigh, NC
Fisk University	1866	Nashville Tenn.
Atlanta University	1867	Atlanta, GA
Virginia Union University	1899	Richmond, VA
Straight University	1869	New Orleans, LA
Talladega College	1867	Talladega, ALA
Clark University	1870	Atlanta, GA
Meharry Medical College	1876	Nashville, TN
Morgan College	1867	Baltimore, MD
New Orleans University	1873	New Orleans, LA
Philander Smith College	1883	Little Rock, ARK
Rust College	1883	Holy Springs, Miss
Samuel Houston College	1900	Austin, TX

Chapter 10

Conclusions

The African American culture did not evolve by accident. It was meticulously developed and designed through the wisdom and leadership of the Black clergy. Using the Bible as their guide, they selected from the western culture those cultural components that they thought were best for their people and built a culture within a culture. The impact they had on the African American cannot be denied or ignored, nor can we ignore the powerful influence that such men and women maintain today.

The Black clergyman was not a magician or a man born with extraordinary power. He was merely an ordinary man who was empowered by his faith in God. Without God, he was hopeless and helpless. The wisdom that he expressed came from God. The courage that he possessed came from God, and the foundation on which he rested came from God.

It was God, through His divine word (the Bible), that inspired the Black clergy to build churches, open up schools and colleges and encourage members to start new businesses. Then God told them to boldly stand up for righteousness and challenge social injustice.

The Black Clergy was the spiritual gardener who planted seeds of righteousness in the fertile hearts of Black men and women. And from those seeds grew a strong culture and a strong people, rooted in righteousness and grounded in God, a people who looked to God for everything and based all of their commitments on *"if it's the Lord's will"* (James 4:15).

Through the planting and pruning of God's Gardener, African Americans blossomed into a beautiful culture, one with strong morals, strong family values and a strong faith in God.

Today, our cultural garden, as we once knew it, is all but destroyed. Many of our spiritual gardeners have lost the art of planting and pruning, while others are trading their pruning shears and plows for politics, and studying preaching no more.

Today, our cultural garden is filled with weeds, weeds that produce gang violence, alcoholism, drugs, teenage pregnancy, and broken homes. The flowers that once blossomed with pride in the African American paradise are now starting to wither while others are being rooted up by non-religious government programs and by ministers who are compromising Godly standards for a status in society. Isaiah referred to these individuals as *"greedy dumb dogs,"* who have lost their boldness to bark (Isaiah 56:10-11).

Our cultural garden doesn't look the same anymore. It seems as if everyone is taking advantage of our cultural experience and planting everything in our garden except those things that made us a strong people. The old time Black minister is **rarely** seen around the garden anymore. He has been replaced with representatives from the women's movement, the gay rights movement, and every other group that has claimed they can identify with us, all planting their own ideas and agendas. There are so many people in our garden, there's hardly room for us, and none are interested in planting our cultural seeds, seeds that produced God-fearing people, strong families and a race of people with high moral standards. The beautiful species we once knew seems to no longer exist.

We must do something and we must do it now. We must learn of our culture before we can appreciate our culture, and we must appreciate our culture before we can preserve our culture. We must not allow others to destroy our cultural beauty, nor can we remain passive and allow others to give us an identity that separates us from the God who has done so much for us (Hosea 6:1).

We must embrace our own beauty and cherish our own identity. We must never allow others to devalue those things that made us so wonderfully unique. And we must never allow others to determine our destiny, when they have never been a part of our dignity.

Appendix 1
Police Records in the Sean Perryman Case

Seattle Police Department
Case Investigation Report

Case Investigation Report: 2015-109387

Certification for Determination of Probable Cause

That **Paul Suguro** is a Detective with the Seattle Police Department and has reviewed the investigation conducted in Seattle Police Department Case number 2015-109387. There is probable cause to believe that **Sean Christian PERRYMAN** committed the crime of Assault within the City of Seattle, County of King, and State of Washington. This belief is predicated on the following facts and circumstances.

On April 4th 2015 at approximately 1:20 AM, Justin ISMAEL, was outside in front of the Rhino Room bar, located at 1535-11th Ave, in the City of Seattle, County of King and State of Washington.

There was a disturbance in front of the Rhino Room involving Matthew TAYLOR and security guards from the Rhino Room. Taylor's friend, Sean Christian PERRYMAN, tried to calm Taylor down. Ismael saw Perryman throw Taylor to the ground.

Ismael intervened in an attempt to calm down Taylor and Perryman. Witnesses said Perryman shoved Ismael, pushing him to the ground. Perryman started attacking Ismael by punching and kicking Ismael.

Rhino Room security guards were able to separate Perryman from Ismael and handcuffed Perryman.

Seattle Police Officers arrived. Ismael identified Perryman to the officers and the one who pushed him to the ground and attacked him. The officers placed Perryman under arrest.

Seattle Fire Department responded and treated Ismael for his injured knee. Ismael was transported to Harborview Medical Center where he was diagnosed with a dislocated left knee. Ismael was treated and released from Harborview Medical Center.

Perryman was transported and booked into King County Jail.

Under penalty of perjury under the laws of the State of Washington, I certify that the foregoing is true and correct to the best of my knowledge and belief. Signed and dated by me this 8th day of April 2015, at Seattle, Washington.

CIR Rev.8/12

SEATTLE POLICE DEPARTMENT
GENERAL OFFENSE HARDCOPY
PUBLIC DISCLOSURE RELEASE COPY

GO# 2015-109387 REFERRED - KCPA - ADULT   1306-0 ASSLT-AGG-BODYFORCE

Related Image - DOCUMENT

Attachment Description: **STATEMENT-OFFICER FRY**
Reference Number:

SEATTLE POLICE DEPARTMENT	**STATEMENT FORM**	GENERAL OFFENSE #	2015-109387
		RELATED EVENTS	

Date: 04/15/2015	Time: 1450	Place: 610 5th Avenue Seattle, WA	
Statement of: ☐ Complainant ☐ Witness ☐ Victim ☒ Officer ☐ Other:			
Name (Last, First MI) Officer Fry, Sonya			DOB
Statement Taken By: Officer Fry		Serial 6838	Unit 3384
Transcribed by (Taped/Translated Statements)		Serial	Unit

On 04/15/2015, I was working a plain clothes assignment with the Seattle Police Department in the Technical and Electronic Support unit. At approximately 1159 hours, I arrived at The Rhino Room located at 1535 11th Ave Seattle, WA to recover video evidence from their surveillance system for Detective P. Suguro.

Detective Suguro of the Homicide Unit requested that I recover surveillance video from all outside cameras for the assault that was committed on 04/04/2015. I contacted and spoke with Patrick who is the owner of The Rhino Room and made the Samsung SDR-5102N2T 16 Channel digital recorder available to me when I arrived today. I verified the date/time stamp on the Samsung digital recorder April 15, 2015 with the time of 11:59 am and the time I had on my work iPhone which was the same.

I verified there were sixteen cameras and nine of them were functional cameras on their surveillance system for the date and time requested above.

Camera #8 – Outside rear door facing north
Camera #9 – Outside camera facing north off the northeast corner of the building

I captured video from all the above listed camera views dated April 4, 2015 from 0100 – 0140 hours. I returned the Rhino Surveillance system back to the live view. I returned to the office and delivered the recovered video evidence to Detective Suguro. That completed my involvement with this incident. I completed this statement. END-OF-STATEMENT.

Witness	
Witness	x S. *My* #6838

Form 9.27 Rev. 11/07   Page 1 of 1

City of Seattle
Seattle Police Department

7/28/2015

Wayne Perryman
P.O. Box 256
Mercer Island, WA 98040

Re: Public Disclosure Appeal – P2015-3597

Dear Mr. Perryman:

The purpose of this correspondence is to provide you with a status update regarding the PDR appeal you filed with the Seattle Police Department Legal Unit. The Legal Unit's administrative review of your appeal is not yet complete. We are currently working with the lead detective to retrieve the record responsive to your request. The detective is out of the office until July 31, 2015.

Consequently, the Legal Unit expects to respond to you on or about August 7, 2015. Thank you for your patience as we work to gather the responsive record.

If you have any questions, please contact the Legal Unit at (206) 684-5757.

Sincerely,

Kathleen O'Toole
Chief of Police

Katie Berger
Legal Unit Manager

Seattle Police Department, 610 Fifth Avenue, PO Box 34986, Seattle, WA 98124-4986
An equal employment opportunity, affirmative action employer.
Accommodations for people with disabilities provided upon request. Call (206) 233-7203 at least two weeks in advance.

Public Disclosure Request
For
Rhino Bar Surveillance Video

On July 30, 2015, at 10:00 AM, Wayne Perryman called Katie Berger the Legal Manager of the Seattle Police Department (206-684-5757) to follow up on his appeal request for the Rhino Bar's surveillance video. Ms Berger reported that the Rhino Bar surveillance video as of July 30, 2015 had not been entered as evidence in this case by the investigative detective (even though the case was dismissed on July 15, 2015).

The original request for this video through Public Disclosure was made on May 7, 2015. The Public Disclosure clerk informed Mr. Perryman that the video was not sent because it had never been entered as evidence. In fact she was unaware that the video even existed. An appeal was filed with Seattle Police's Legal Department on June 12, 2015, requesting a copy of the video.

1

2 **FILED**
KING COUNTY, WASHINGTON

3 JUL 1 6 2015

4 SUPERIOR COURT CLERK

5

6 SUPERIOR COURT OF WASHINGTON FOR KING COUNTY

7

8 STATE OF WASHINGTON,)
)
9 Plaintiff,) No. 15-1-02418-0 SEA
)
10 vs.)
) MOTION, CERTIFICATION AND
11 SEAN CHRISTIAN PERRYMAN,) ORDER OF DISMISSAL
) [Clerk's Action Required]
12 Defendant.)
)
13)

14 COMES NOW Daniel T. Satterberg, Prosecuting Attorney for King County, Washington,
by and through his deputy, and moves the court for an order dismissing the above-entitled cause
15 as to the above defendant for the reasons as set forth in the certification of the undersigned
deputy prosecuting attorney.
16
I am a Senior Deputy Prosecuting Attorney in and for King County, Washington, and am
17 familiar with the records and files herein. This case should be dismissed for the following
reasons: The State has received additional evidence since the case was filed that impacts the
18 State's ability to proceed with prosecution. Given these evidentiary issues, this case should be
dismissed in the administration of justice.
19
Under penalty of perjury under the laws of the State of Washington, I certify that the foregoing is
20 true and correct. Signed and dated by me this ___16th___ day of July, 2015, at Seattle, Washington.

21

22

23

24
Julie D. Cook, WSBA #28271
MOTION, CERTIFICATION AND ORDER OF   Daniel T. Satterberg, Prosecuting Attorney
DISMISSAL - 1   Criminal Division
                                       W554 King County Courthouse
                                       516 Third Avenue
                                       Seattle, WA 98104-2385
                                       (206) 296-9000 FAX (206) 296-0955

1 Senior Deputy Prosecuting Attorney

<u>ORDER</u>

2

3   IT APPEARING from the motion and certification that the ends of justice do not warrant
further proceedings in this matter; now, therefore
      IT IS HEREBY ORDERED, ADJUDGED and DECREED that the above-entitled cause

4 as to the above named defendant be, and the same hereby is, dismissed.
      DONE IN OPEN COURT this __16__ day of July, 2015.

5

6   JUDGE

7 Presented by:

8

9

10 Julie D. Cook, WSBA# 28271
Senior Deputy Prosecuting Attorney

11

12

13

14

15

16

17

18

19

20

21

22

23

24

MOTION, CERTIFICATION AND ORDER OF
DISMISSAL - 2

Daniel T. Satterberg, Prosecuting Attorney
Criminal Division
W554 King County Courthouse
516 Third Avenue
Seattle, WA 98104-2385
(206) 296-9000 FAX (206) 296-0955

Appendix 2

Background on Sean Perryman

July 9, 2014

Sean Perryman
PO Box 256
Mercer Island, WA 98040-0256

Dear Sean:

Congratulations! Your academic excellence has placed you on the Dean's List in the College of Education and Professional Studies for Spring Quarter 2014. Achievement of the Dean's List is a significant accomplishment. Dean's Lists are widely recognized throughout higher education as a standard of scholastic excellence.

The faculty and staff at Central Washington University take sincere pride in your success. Your dedication to learning and your willingness to expend the effort required in scholarly endeavors are impressive. It is with great pleasure that we include you on the Dean's List and we challenge you to maintain this level of excellence throughout your academic pursuits.

Please share this honor with your family so that they may join us in congratulating you for this achievement!

Sincerely,

Connie Lambert, Dean
College of Education and Professional Studies

The National Society of Collegiate Scholars

To all who read these letters

~ Greetings ~

The Honorary Board of Regents and the Board of Directors
of The National Society of Collegiate Scholars confer honor and distinction upon

Sean Christian Perryman

for commitment to the ideals of

Scholarship, Leadership and Service

Presented on February 2, 2015

With this recognition comes all the rights, honors and privileges thereunto pertaining to the Society at

Central Washington University

Founder and Chief Executive Officer

Advisor

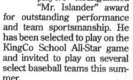

A10 Mercer Island Reporter · Wednesday, June 4, 2008

Islanders honored

Perryman receives Lincoln Award

The Mercer Island Republican Women are proud to honor Sean Perryman with the 11th annual Lincoln Award. Perryman will receive a $1,000 college scholarship and "Words Lincoln Lived By," a book about Lincoln. His name will be posted on the Lincoln Award Plaque at Mercer Island High School, and he will be recognized at the high school's Awards Breakfast on June 6. Perryman's winning essay, titled "The Separation of Church and State," addresses religious liberty as intended by the founders as opposed to the more recent reinterpretation of Thomas Jefferson's letter to the Danbury Church.

The Lincoln Award is given to further students' knowledge of U.S. history, recognize outstanding student scholarship

Sean Perryman

and encourage independent thinking. The winner is selected after students submit an essay that is reviewed by a MIRW committee. This year, the committee received a record number of essays.

Perryman received the 2008 Mercer Island Community Scholarship Award from the Mercer Island PTA Council for outstanding attitude, effort and achievement for a social studies scholarship. He also received the MIHS baseball coaches and players distinguished "Mr. Islander" award for outstanding performance and team sportsmanship. He has been selected to play on the KingCo School All-Star game and invited to play on several select baseball teams this summer.

Perryman is the son of Rev. Wayne Perryman

He has worked on a multitude of community service and fundraising projects since he was 7 years old, including a project to build a teen center for inner city teens with his father. He has helped the needy during the holiday season and raised money for African children who were victimized by war.

Perryman will attend Westmont College in Santa Barbara, Calif., this fall, where he plans to major in business and marketing, and join the college baseball team.

Complete Report

Request #: EX-072815-G874J
Turnaround time: 2.9 business days
Passport Unlimited, Inc
801 Kirkland Ave
Kirkland, WA 98033
Phone: (425) 952-5383

HireRight, Inc.
3349 Michelson Dr. Suite 150
Irvine, CA 92612
Phone: 800-490-7983
Fax: 877-797-3442
ExpressSupport@hireright.com

Requested By: Cindy McDonald
Phone: (425) 952-5383
E-mail: cindym@passportunlimited.com
Date Request Submitted: 07/28/2015 02:07:29 PM PDT
Request Completion Date: 07/31/2015 12:29:23 PM PDT
Package: ADVANTAGE PLUS

Applicant's Personal Information

Sean Christian Perryman
DOB: **/**/****
USA   Social Security Number: ***-**-9012

Results Summary

Verification	Status	Discrepancy
SSN Validation	Complete	No
Court Records	Complete	Yes
Address History	Complete	No
National Sex Offender Registry	Complete	No
National Crim Search	Complete	No

Sean Perryman, ***-**-9012 – Completed 7/31/2015 12:29 PM

———————————— Court Records ————————————

2 subrequests

1. Criminal Felony & Misdemeanor   Complete – No Court Record Found
(Past 7 Years Search)
Perryman, Sean

Address(es): Smithfield, Johnston County, NC, USA

Location Searched:	**Smithfield, Johnston County, NC**
Time Completed:	07/28/2015 05:15:40 PM PDT
Verified by:	QA–434

Comments: 07/28/2015 02:07:30 PM PDT – Note:
————Reason: Johnston County, NC – Average court turnaround time
is currently 2 business days.

2. Criminal Felony & Misdemeanor (Past 7 Years Search)   Complete – Court Record
Perryman, Sean   Found

Address(es): Mercer Island, King County, WA, USA

Location Searched:	**Mercer Island, King County, WA**
Time Completed:	07/31/2015 12:29:22 PM PDT
Verified by:	QA–33764

Comments: 07/28/2015 02:07:29 PM PDT – Note:
————Reason: King County, WA – Average court turnaround time is currently 2
business days.

07/29/2015 10:24:36 AM PDT – Anitha, Lingadhari – Note: Name on record
confirmed to match the applicant

1.) Case Nbr.: 15–1–02418–0 (King County)
Comments:
Identifiers: Confirmation: Name, Date Of Birth. Name on File: PERRYMAN, SEAN CHRISTIAN

Count:	1	**Severity:**	Felony class C
Offense Date:	04/08/2015	**Disp. Date:**	07/16/2015
Offense:	ASSAULT–3RD DEGREE SUBSTANTIAL PAIN		
Disposition:	Dismissed		
Sentence:			

Sean Perryman, ***–**–9012 – Completed 7/31/2015 12:29 PM

——————————— SSN Validation   ————————————

Results: SSN ***–**–9012 was issued in 1990–1991 in WASHINGTON. SSN   Complete – SSN has been
is not in the death index.   issued by the SSA

[1] "Complete" indicates that this request has been processed to conclusion. Please review the report details in their entirety to evaluate any potential discrepancies or records related to this request.

All times listed in Pacific – USA timezone

LEGAL NOTES:
The information provided herein is a consumer report as defined in the federal Fair Credit Reporting Act [15 USC 1681 et.seq.] It contains confidential information on the individual named. It is submitted subject to the express conditions contained in your Subscriber Agreement with HireRight, and may be used solely for legally permissible employment purposes (i.e., as a factor in evaluating the named individual for employment, promotion, reassignment or retention as an employee). Proper use of the content of this report and final verification of the named individual's identity is your sole responsibility.

Appendix 3
Wall Street Journal and EEOC Policy

As Arrest Records Rise, Americans Find Consequences Can Last a Lif...

DOW JONES, A NEWS CORP COMPANY ▾

Nikkei ▲ 20047.64 0.13%   Hang Seng ▲ 26672.16 0.56%   U.S. 10 Yr ▲ 1/32 Yield 2.269%

THE WALL STREET JOURNAL.

http://www.wsj.com/articles/as-arrest-records-rise-americans-find-consequences-can-last-a-lifetime-1408415402

U.S. NEWS

As Arrest Records Rise, Americans Find Consequences Can Last a Lifetime

Even if Charges Were Dropped, a Lingering Arrest Record Can Ruin Chances of a Job

Jose Gabriel Hernandez was arrested after being falsely identified as a sexual predator. BEN SKLAR FOR THE WALL STREET JOURNAL

By Gary Fields and John R. Emshwiller
Aug. 18, 2014 10:30 p.m. ET

America has a rap sheet.

Over the past 20 years, authorities have made more than a quarter of a billion arrests, the Federal Bureau of Investigation estimates. As a result, the FBI currently has 77.7 million individuals on file in its master criminal database—or nearly one out of every three American adults.

> Between 10,000 and 12,000 new names are added each day.

At the same time, an information explosion has made it easy for anyone to pull up arrest records in an instant. Employers, banks, college admissions officers and landlords, among others, routinely check records online. The information doesn't typically describe what happened next.

Many people who have never faced charges, or have had charges dropped, find that a lingering arrest record can ruin their chance to secure employment, loans and housing. Even in cases of a mistaken arrest, the damaging documents aren't automatically removed. In other instances, arrest information is forwarded to the FBI but not necessarily updated there when a case is thrown out locally. Only half of the records with the FBI have fully up-to-date information.

"There is a myth that if you are arrested and cleared that it has no impact," says Paul Butler, professor of law at Georgetown Law. "It's not like the arrest never happened."

Precious Daniels of Detroit is part of a class-action lawsuit against the Census Bureau alleging that tens of thousands of African-Americans were discriminated against because of the agency's use of arrest records in its hiring process. FABRIZIO COSTANTINI FOR THE WALL STREET JOURNAL

When Precious Daniels learned that the Census Bureau was looking for temporary workers, she thought she would make an ideal candidate. The lifelong Detroit resident and veteran health-care worker knew the people in the community. She had studied psychology at a local college.

Days after she applied for the job in 2010, she received a letter indicating a routine background check had turned up a red flag.

In November of 2009, Ms. Daniels had participated in a protest against Blue Cross Blue Shield of Michigan as the health-care law was being debated. Arrested with others for disorderly conduct, she was released on $50 bail and the misdemeanor charge was subsequently dropped. Ms. Daniels didn't anticipate any further problems.

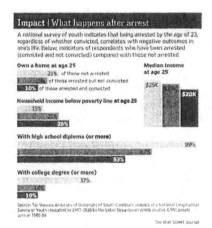

But her job application brought the matter back to life. For the application to proceed, the Census bureau informed her she would need to submit fingerprints and gave her 30 days to obtain court documents proving her case had been resolved without a conviction.

Clearing her name was easier said than done. "From what I was told by the courthouse, they didn't have a record," says Ms. Daniels, now 39 years old. She didn't get the job. Court officials didn't respond to requests for comment.

Today, Ms. Daniels is part of a class-action lawsuit against the Census Bureau alleging that tens of thousands of African-Americans were discriminated against because of the agency's use of arrest records in its hiring process. Adam Klein, a New York-based plaintiff attorney, says a total of about 850,000 applicants received similar letters to the one sent to Ms. Daniels.

Representatives for the Census Bureau and the U.S. Justice Department declined to comment. In court filings, the government denied the discrimination allegation and said plaintiffs' method for analyzing hiring data was "unreliable" and "statistically invalid."

MORE

• Permanent Record: How Arrests Stick With Tens of Millions of Americans

The wave of arrests has been fueled in part by unprecedented federal dollars funneled to local police departments and new policing tactics that condoned arrests for even the smallest offenses. Spending on law-enforcement by states and local governments hit $212 billion in 2011, including judicial, police and corrections costs, according to the most recent estimates provided to the U.S. Census Bureau. By comparison, those figures, when adjusted for inflation, were equivalent to $179 billion in 2001 and $128 billion in 1992.

In 2011, the most recent year for which figures are available, the Bureau of Justice Statistics put the number of full-time equivalent sworn state and local police officers at 646,213—up from 531,706 in 1991.

A crackdown on what seemed like an out-of-control crime rate in the late 1980s and early 1990s made sense at the time, says Jack Levin, co-director of the Brudnick Center on Violence and Conflict at Boston's Northeastern University.

"Zero-tolerance policing spread across the country after the 1990s because of the terrible crime problem in late '80s and early 1990s," says Mr. Levin.

The push to put an additional 100,000 more officers on the streets in the 1990s focused on urban areas where the crime rates were the highest, says Mr. Levin.

And there has been success, he says, as crime rates have fallen and the murder rate has dropped.

But as a consequence, "you've got these large numbers of people now who are stigmatized," he says. "The impact of so many arrests is catastrophic."

That verdict isn't unanimous. "We made arrests for minor infractions that deterred the more serious infractions down the road," says James Pasco, executive director of the Fraternal Order of Police, which represents about 335,000 officers. "We don't apologize for that. Innocent people are alive today and kids have grown up to lead productive lives because of the actions people took in those days."

At the University of South Carolina, researchers have been examining other national data in an attempt to understand the long-term impact of arrests on young people. Using information from a 16-year-long U.S. Bureau of Labor Statistics survey, researchers tracked 7,335 randomly selected people into their 20s, scrutinizing subjects for any brushes with the law.

Researchers report that more than 40% of the male subjects have been arrested at least once by the age of 23. The rate was highest for blacks, at 49%, 44% for Hispanics and 38% for whites. Researchers found that nearly one in five women had been arrested at least once by the age of 23.

They further determined that 47% of those arrested weren't convicted. In more than a quarter of cases, subjects weren't even formally charged.

Mr. Hernandez carries a laminated legal document from the Bexar County Sheriff's office confirming his innocence in case he is arrested in the future. BEN SKLAR FOR THE WALL STREET JOURNAL

It can be daunting to try to correct the record. In October 2012, Jose Gabriel Hernandez was finishing up dinner at home when officers came to arrest him for sexually assaulting two young girls.

Turns out, it was a case of mistaken identity. In court documents, the prosecutor's office acknowledged that the "wrong Jose Hernandez" had been arrested and the charges were dropped.

Once the case was dismissed, Mr. Hernandez assumed authorities would set the record straight. Instead, he learned that the burden was on him to clear his record and that he would need a lawyer to seek a formal expungement.

"Needless to say, that hasn't happened yet," says Mr. Hernandez, who works as a contractor. Mr. Hernandez was held in the Bexar County jail on $150,000 bond. He didn't have the cash, so his wife borrowed money to pay a bail bondsman the nonrefundable sum of $22,500, or the 15% fee, he needed to put up. They are still repaying the loans.

Exacerbating the situation are for-profit websites and other background-check businesses that assemble publicly available arrest records, often including mug shots and charges. Many sites charge fees to remove a record, even an outdated or erroneous one. In the past year Google Inc. has changed its search algorithm to de-emphasize many so called "mug-shot" websites, giving them less prominence when someone's name is searched.

On Friday, California Gov. Jerry Brown signed into law a bill making it illegal for websites to charge state residents to have their mug shot arrest photos removed.

In 2013, Indiana legislators approved one of the most extensive criminal record expungement laws in the country. The law was sponsored by a former prosecutor and had a range of conservative Republican backers. One had worked as a mining-company supervisor who frequently had to reject individuals after routine background checks found evidence of an old arrest.

"If we are going to judge people, we need to judge them on who they are now, and not who they were," says Jud McMillin, the bill's chief sponsor.

The "growing obsession with background checking and commercial exploitation of arrest and conviction records makes it all but impossible for someone with a criminal record to leave the past behind," concludes a recent report from the National Association of Criminal Defense Lawyers.

Further analysis by the University of South Carolina team, performed at the request of The Wall Street Journal, suggests that men with arrest records—even absent a formal charge or conviction—go on to earn lower salaries. They are also less likely to own a home compared with people who have never been arrested.

The same holds true for graduation rates and whether a person will live below the poverty line.

For example, more than 95% of subjects without arrests in the survey graduated high school or earned an equivalent diploma. The number falls to 84.4% for those who were arrested and yet not convicted.

Tia Stevens Andersen, the University of South Carolina researcher who performed the analysis, says the results are consistent with what criminologists have found. The data, especially when coupled with other studies, show that an arrest "does have a substantial impact on people's lives," she says. That is in part because "it's now cheap and easy to do a background check."

According to a 2012 survey by the Society for Human Resource Management, 69% of employers conduct criminal background checks on all job applicants. Fewer than that—about 58%—allow candidates to explain any negative results of a check.

Mike Mitternight, the owner and president of Factory Service Agency Inc., a heating and air-conditioning company in Metairie, La., worries that if he turns down a job applicant because of a criminal record, he could be open to a discrimination claim. But hiring the person could leave him open to liability if something goes wrong. "I have to do the background checks and take my chances," says Mr. Mitternight. "It's a lose-lose situation."

John Keir says he was fired from his job after failing to mention brushes with the law on his application. Found not guilty of a recent charge, he says he answered truthfully. STEVE GATES FOR THE WALL STREET JOURNAL

John and Jessica Keir, of Birmingham, Ala., have tried various means to combat their arrest stigma. In 2012 the married couple was accused of criminal mischief for scratching someone's car with a key. They were found not guilty at trial.

In January of last year, Ms. Keir, a law-school student, googled herself. "My mug shot was everywhere," she recalls. "I was just distraught."

Though she was in the top 15% of her first-year class at Cumberland School of Law School in Birmingham, she says about a dozen law firms turned her down for summer work. Since she rarely made it to the interview stage, she feared her online mug shots played a role. Eventually, she landed a summer position at the Alabama attorney general's office.

The couple says they paid about $2,000 to various websites to remove their mug shots. It didn't work, Mr. Keir says. New mug-shot sites seemed to appear almost daily. Keeping up with them all was "like playing Whac-A-Mole," says Mr. Keir.

Ms. Keir, who is finishing her law degree at the University of Alabama, has been using Facebook, LinkedIn and Google to create enough positive Internet traffic to try to push down negative information lower in any search-engine results.

Meanwhile, her husband believes he has been caught up in a separate quagmire. Earlier this year Mr. Keir was hired by Regions Bank as an information security official. Weeks later, he says he was let go from his $85,000 job for allegedly lying on his application.

The 35-year-old Mr. Keir says his firing resulted after failing to disclose his recent arrest record as well as a number of traffic violations during his teens that had branded him as a "youthful offender" in Alabama. He says he didn't lie on his application, and only recalls being asked about any criminal convictions.

A spokeswoman for Regions Bank, a unit of Regions Financial Corp., says the company couldn't discuss individual personnel matters, but says the bank sends applicant fingerprints to the FBI as part of criminal background check and asks candidates to answer questions about previous criminal charges and convictions.

Arrest issues don't necessarily abate with age.

Barbara Ann Finn lost out on a school cafeteria job last year after a background check turned up a 1963 hit on her record, which was a surprise to her. GREG KENDALL-BALL FOR THE WALL STREET JOURNAL

Late last year, Barbara Ann Finn, a 74-year-old great grandmother, applied for a part-time job as a cafeteria worker in the Worcester County, Md., school system.

"I was a single woman on a fixed income. I was trying to help myself," she recalls.

Along with the application came fingerprints and other checks—a process Ms. Finn dismissed as mere formality. After all, she had lived in the area since 1985, had worked in various parts of county government and served as a foster parent. Her background had been probed before.

So she was surprised by the phone call she received from the school district. Her fingerprints, she says she was told, had been run through both the state and FBI criminal databases. She was clear in Maryland, but the FBI check matched her prints to a 1963 arrest of someone with a name she says she doesn't recognize.

Barbara Witherow, a spokeswoman with the school district, confirms that Ms. Finn had applied for employment and that there were "valid reasons why" she

NOTICE Number *EEOC* 915.061 **Date** 9/7/90

1. SUBJECT: Policy Guidance on the Consideration of **Arrest Records in Employment Decisions under Title VII of the Civil Rights Act of 1964, as amended, 42 U.S.C. §2000e et seq. (1982).**
2. PURPOSE: This policy guidance sets forth the Commission's procedure for determining whether arrest records may be considered in employment decisions.
3. EFFECTIVE DATE: Upon Receipt.
4. EXPIRATION DATE: As an exception to EEOC Order 205.001, Appendix B, Attachment 4, §a(5), this Notice will remain in effect until rescinded or superseded.
5. ORIGINATOR: Title VII/EPA Division, Office of the Legal Counsel.
6. INSTRUCTIONS: File behind the last Policy Guidance §604 of Volume II of Compliance Manual.
7. SUBJECT MATTER:

I. Introduction

The question addressed in this policy guidance is "to what extent may **arrest records be used in making employment decisions?**" The Commission concludes that since the use of arrest records as an absolute bar to employment has a disparate impact on some protected groups, such records alone cannot be used to routinely exclude persons from employment. However, conduct which indicates unsuitability for a particular position is a basis for exclusion. Where it appears that the applicant or employee engaged in the conduct for which he was arrested and that the conduct is job-related and relatively recent, exclusion is justified.

The analysis set forth in this policy guidance is related to two previously issued policy statements regarding the consideration of conviction records in employment decisions: "Policy Statement on the Issue of Conviction Records under Title VII of the Civil Rights Act of 1964, as amended 42 U.S.C. §2000e *et seq.* (1982)" (hereinafter referred to as the February 4, 1987 Statement) and "Policy Statement on the use of statistics in charges involving the exclusion of individuals with conviction records from employment" (hereinafter referred to as July 29, 1987 Statement). The February 4, 1987 Statement states that nationally, Blacks and Hispanics are convicted in numbers which are disproportionate to Whites and that barring people from employment based on their conviction records will therefore disproportionately exclude those groups.[1] Due to this adverse impact, an employer may not base an employment decision on the conviction record of an applicant or an employee absent business necessity.[2] **Business necessity can be established where the employee or applicant is engaged in conduct which is particularly egregious or related to the position in question.**

Appendix 4

US Attorney Jenny Durkan's Briefs
agianst Seattle Police

1

HON._____

2

3

4

5

6

UNITED STATES DISTRICT COURT

7 WESTERN DISTRICT OF WASHINGTON
   AT SEATTLE

8

UNITED STATES OF AMERICA,	12-CV-_____
9 Plaintiff,	
10	**COMPLAINT**
v.	
11	
CITY OF SEATTLE,	
12	
Defendant.	

13

Plaintiff the United States of America ("United States") brings this civil cause of action

14

against Defendant the City of Seattle (the "City" or "Seattle") under the Violent Crime Control

15

and Law Enforcement Act of 1994, 42 U.S.C. § 14141.

16

The United States brings this action to remedy a pattern or practice of conduct by law

17

enforcement officers of the Seattle Police Department ("SPD" or "the Department"), an agent of

18

the City, that deprives persons of rights, privileges, and immunities secured and protected by the

19

Constitution and the law of the United States.

20

The United States alleges as follows:

21

I.   JURISDICTION AND VENUE

22

1.   This Court has jurisdiction of this action under 28 U.S.C. §§ 1331, 1345

23

and 2201.

COMPLAINT - 1
12-CV-

1   37.   SPD has not only failed to properly supervise individual use of force incidents,

2 but has also engaged in a widespread failure to effectively monitor officers who use force

3 repeatedly.

4   38.   SPD's Early Intervention System ("EIS") does not serve as a meaningful

5 mechanism for either mentoring/training officers or for identifying and curbing officers' use of

6 force problems. For example, in one 14-month period, an officer participated in 20 uses of force

7 and was the subject of four OPA complaints regarding his use of force. This led to four EIS

8 interventions where supervisors were required to review the officer's use of force reports and

9 identify any problematic behavior or issues that flag training or tactical questions. No issues

10 were identified by the supervisors for the 20 uses of force. Instead, during each intervention, the

11 reviewing supervisor approved the officer's use of force, without providing any additional

12 training or tactical suggestions to avoid uses of force.

13   39.   DOJ's investigation revealed that these failures are not isolated; SPD routinely

14 failed to identify patterns of excessive force and take adequate measures to prevent their

15 recurrence.

16   40.   Similarly, SPD's OPA system has not provided the intended backstop for the

17 failures of the direct supervisory review process. For years, SPD disposed of nearly two-thirds

18 of citizens' complaints by sending them to SPD's precincts, where the quality of investigations is

19 deficient, and where SPD provided no additional monitoring for alleged attempts to provide

20 remedial training or other interventions for officers.

21   41.   SPD's failure to supervise means that SPD leadership is unaware of which of its

22 officers use force frequently, or why. In 2010, just 20 officers (four percent of its officers) used

23 force seven or more times, participating in eighteen percent of the acknowledged use of force

COMPLAINT - 11
12-CV-

1 situations and the failure to report uses of force. SPD has not made substantial progress towards

2 implementing any of the recommendations made by OPA.

3   46.   Further, SPD knew or should have known of its deficient policies, supervision,

4 training, and procedures through the lawsuits the City has litigated and settled. The City has

5 spent millions of dollars in attorneys' fees defending police misconduct cases. In the last six

6 years, it has paid approximately $3 million in settlements, verdicts and attorneys fees to

7 plaintiffs. Many of these cases have provided the City with notice of, and are further evidence,

8 of, the pattern or practice alleged herein.

9   47.   In short, SPD knew or should have known that its policies or practices,

10 particularly its inadequate policies, training, supervision, and practices, would inevitably cause

11 Fourth Amendment violations.

12   48.   Despite these clear warnings, SPD has failed to implement policies, systems of

13 supervision, adequate training or procedures that will protect against uses of excessive force.

14 The fact that these institutional failures and constitutional violations persist, despite SPD's

15 awareness of its deficiencies and officer use of force problems, demonstrates SPD's indifference

16 to the risk of excessive force.

17   **IV.   CLAIM FOR RELIEF: DEFENDANT'S CONDUCT**

18   **VIOLATES § 14141 AND THE FOURTH AMENDMENT**

19   49.   The United States re-alleges and incorporates by reference the allegations set

20 forth above.

21   50.   Defendant engages in law enforcement practices that result in excessive force

22 against persons in Seattle.

23

UNITED STATES ATTORNEY
700 Stewart Street, Suite 5220
Seattle, WA 98101-1271
(206) 553-7970

1 c.   Policies, procedures, training, and supervision to address issues of

2   discriminatory policing, including prohibiting the use of racially charged

3   language directed towards individuals;

4 d.   Policies, procedures, training, and supervision regarding crisis

5   intervention, social contact, and investigatory stops, and strategies to

6   prevent discriminatory policing; and

7 e.   Accountability measures to hold officers and supervisors accountable for

8   uses of excessive force and discriminatory policing.

9 56. Order such other appropriate relief as the interests of justice may require.

10   Respectfully submitted on July 27, 2012.

11

12 For the UNITED STATES OF AMERICA:

13 ERIC H. HOLDER, JR.
    Attorney General of the United States of America

14

15 /s/ Jenny A. Durkan   /s/ Thomas E. Perez
    JENNY A. DURKAN   THOMAS E. PEREZ
16 United States Attorney for the   Assistant Attorney General
    Western District of Washington   Civil Rights Division

17
    Kerry J. Keefe, Civil Chief   Jonathan M. Smith, Chief
18 J. Michael Diaz, Assistant United States Attorney   Timothy D. Mygatt, Special Counsel
    Rebecca S. Cohen, Assistant United States Attorney   Michelle L. Leung, Trial Attorney
19 United States Attorney's Office   Michael J. Songer, Trial Attorney
    Western District of Washington   United States Department of Justice
20 700 Stewart Street, Suite 5220   Civil Rights Division
    Seattle, Washington 98101-1271   Special Litigation Section
21 Phone: (206) 553-7970   950 Pennsylvania Avenue, NW
    Fax: (206) 553-4073   Washington, DC 20530
22 E-mail: Michael.Diaz@usdoj.gov   Phone: (202) 514-6255
                                                           Fax: (202) 514-4883
23   E-mail: Michelle.Leung@usdoj.gov

COMPLAINT - 15
12-CV-

Case 2:12-cv-01282-JLR Document 5 Filed 08/17/12 Page 1 of 12

1   The Honorable James L. Robart

2

3

4

5

6   UNITED STATES DISTRICT COURT
                   WESTERN DISTRICT OF WASHINGTON

7   AT SEATTLE

8   UNITED STATES OF AMERICA,   12-CV-1282-JLR

9   Plaintiff,   STIPULATION AND JOINT [PROPOSED]
                                    FINDINGS OF FACT AND

10   v.   CONCLUSIONS OF LAW

11   CITY OF SEATTLE,   Please Note on Motion Calendar for:
                                    August 17, 2012

12   Defendant.

13   Pursuant to Fed. R. Civ. P. 52, the City of Seattle ("the City") and the United States of

14 America ("the United States") (collectively "the Parties") hereby stipulate to, and jointly and

15 respectfully submit, the following [Proposed] Findings of Fact and Conclusions of Law.

16   **[PROPOSED] FINDINGS OF FACT AND CONCLUSIONS OF LAW**

17   **I.**   **INTRODUCTION**

18   The Parties' (1) Joint Motion and [Proposed] Order for Approval of Settlement

19 Agreement and Stipulated Order of Resolution and Entry of Judgment (Dkt. No. 3, filed July 27,

20 2012, "Joint Motion") and (2) Stipulation and Joint [Proposed] Findings of Facts and

21 Conclusions of Law (Dkt. No. 5, filed August 17, 2012) were heard in open court on August 24,

22 2012 before the Honorable James L. Robart, United States District Court Judge. Having

23 considered the foregoing and all the documents in the record, including but not limited to the

JOINT [PROPOSED] FINDINGS OF FACT AND CONCLUSIONS OF LAW - 1
12-CV-1282-JLRRBL.

1 Complaint (Dkt. No. 1), and its exhibit thereto (Dkt. No. 1-1, adopted by reference pursuant to

2 Fed. R. Civ. P. 10(c)); having heard and considered the argument of counsel at the publicly-

3 noticed, above-referenced hearing; having further considered the pertinent governing law; and

4 having reviewed the facts and records of this action, the Court makes the following findings of

5 fact and conclusions of law, pursuant to Fed. R. Civ. P. 52(a)(3):

6 **II.   FINDINGS OF FACT**

7 1.   On March 31, 2011, the United States' Department of Justice ("DOJ") publicly

8 announced that it had begun an investigation of the Seattle Police Department ("SPD") pursuant

9 to, *inter alia*, the Violent Crime Control and Law Enforcement Act of 1994, 42 U.S.C. § 14141

10 ("Section 14141"). DOJ's investigative team consisted of lawyers and other staff from the Civil

11 Rights Division and the United States Attorney's Office for the Western District of Washington,

12 working closely with policing consultants.

13 2.   The City and SPD fully cooperated with the investigation.

14 3.   During this nine-month investigation, DOJ and its police experts gathered

15 information through interviews and meetings with SPD officers, supervisors, and command staff,

16 representatives of the Seattle Police Officers' Guild and Seattle Police Management Association,

17 members of the public, City and State officials, and other community stakeholders. The

18 investigation also included on and off-site review of documents, and on-site tours in which DOJ

19 personnel and experts accompanied SPD officers during their shifts.

20 4.   As part of the investigation, DOJ received or reviewed hundreds of thousands of

21 pages of documents, including SPD policies and procedures, training materials, SPD's internal

22 use of force reports, SPD's public reports, files from SPD's Office of Professional

23

JOINT [PROPOSED] FINDINGS OF FACT AND CONCLUSIONS OF LAW - 2
12-CV-1282-JLRRBL

UNITED STATES ATTORNEY
700 Stewart Street, Suite 5220
Seattle, WA 98101-1271
(206) 553-7970

1 Accountability ("OPA"), and community and other publicly available documents, as well as

2 video and other data generated from SPD and OPA databases.

3   5.   The investigation also included hundreds of interviews and meetings with SPD

4 officers, supervisors, command staff, its Auditors past and present, and representatives of the

5 Seattle Police Officers' Guild and Seattle Police Management Association, as well as Seattle

6 City officials, local community advocates and attorneys, and members of the Seattle community

7 at large. DOJ hosted multiple full days of interviews with community members.

8   6.   On December 16, 2011, DOJ released its report ("DOJ Report," Dkt. No. 1-1)

9 announcing that it had found reasonable cause, under Section 14141, to believe that SPD had

10 engaged in a pattern or practice of excessive force. Specifically, the 67-page DOJ Report

11 asserted that SPD had engaged in unjustified use of impact weapons, unjustified escalation of

12 minor encounters into force events particularly against individuals with mental illness or those

13 under the influence of alcohol or drugs, unjustified use of force against persons who were

14 restrained or simply exercising their First Amendment rights, and unjustified use of force by

15 multiple officers. The DOJ Report also asserted that this pattern or practice of using unlawful

16 force derived from SPD's systematic failure to implement adequate policies, procedures,

17 training, and oversight.

18   7.   Although DOJ did not make a finding that SPD engages in a pattern or practice of

19 discriminatory policing, the DOJ Report identified DOJ's serious concerns about certain

20 practices that could have a disparate impact on minority communities and could support

21 allegations of discriminatory policing, including the DOJ finding that over half of the excessive

22 force cases identified by DOJ involved minorities. The United States asserts that many of the

23

1   issues related to discriminatory policing are both aggravated by and contribute to the issues

2   regarding the excessive use of force.

3   8.   The City disputed the findings in the DOJ Report. The City did not admit that

4   any complaint reviewed by DOJ was meritorious or improperly addressed by SPD. The parties

5   agreed that nothing in the settlement agreement or the negotiations would be construed as an

6   admission of wrongdoing by the City or evidence of liability under any federal, state or

7   municipal law.

8   9.   Based on its investigation, DOJ believed it was authorized, under Section 14141,

9   to file a civil action to obtain appropriate equitable and declaratory relief to eliminate the alleged

10   pattern or practice of unlawful use of force, and did initiate a lawsuit pursuant to Section 14141

11   in this Court (Dkt. No. 1).

12   10.   Shortly after DOJ issued its Report, the Parties began negotiations to resolve the

13   United States' concerns without the need to resort to contested litigation.

14   11.   In January and February 2012, DOJ met with the City's elected officials,

15   including its Mayor, City Attorney, and City Council. During the course of approximately seven

16   months, the Parties conducted extensive negotiations over potential revisions to SPD's policies,

17   procedures, and supervisory practices that would prevent a pattern or practice of constitutional

18   violations as alleged by the United States.

19   12.   On March 30, 2012, the United States provided the City with its draft proposed

20   Reform Plan. The City responded with its counter-proposal on May 16, 2012. The Parties

21   subsequently exchanged multiple drafts of proposals and counter-proposals and conducted

22   numerous negotiating sessions. The parties then engaged a professional, licensed mediator who

23   facilitated approximately 100 hours of intense, contested negotiations, which yielded the

JOINT [PROPOSED] FINDINGS OF FACT AND CONCLUSIONS OF LAW - 4
12-CV-1282-JLRRBL

Case 2:12-cv-01282-JLR   Document 5   Filed 08/17/12   Page 5 of 12

1 Settlement Agreement and Stipulated Order of Resolution ("Agreement and Stipulated Order,"

2 Dkt. 2-1), filed in this Court on July 27, 2012.

3   13.   During this process, both the United States and the City consulted with subject

4 matter experts, both internal and external, to ensure that the remedial measures in the Agreement

5 and Stipulated Order are tailored to address the specific concerns identified by DOJ and can be

6 reasonably implemented by SPD. SPD command staff, OPA, and other SPD personnel assisted

7 in crafting the Agreement and Stipulated Order and in resolving potential adverse operational

8 impacts.

9   14.   The Parties are sophisticated and were represented by experienced counsel. The

10 parties are intimately familiar with SPD's policies and practices and invested significant time

11 negotiating the Agreement and Stipulated Order.

12   15.   Additionally, since the beginning of 2012, DOJ conducted extensive outreach to

13 SPD, its officers, supervisors, and command staff, the Seattle Police Officers' Guild and Seattle

14 Police Management Association, and OPA and its former and current civilian Auditors. *See*

15 Declaration of J. Michael Diaz, filed herewith. Both parties reached out to members of the

16 public, City and State officials, and many community stakeholders, including community

17 advocacy organizations, and minority and ethnic community organizations. *Id.* The Parties

18 received multiple detailed written recommendations from community organizations. *Id.*

19 Through this outreach, the Parties sought to solicit and did incorporate, as appropriate, the input

20 of individuals and organizations into the Agreement and Stipulated Order. *Id.*

21   16.   The express purpose of the Agreement and Stipulated Order was to resolve the

22 litigation filed by the United States and to ensure that police services are delivered to the Seattle

23 community in a manner that fully complies with the Constitution and laws of the United States.

JOINT [PROPOSED] FINDINGS OF FACT AND CONCLUSIONS OF LAW - 5
12-CV-1282-JLRRBI.

UNITED STATES ATTORNEY
700 Stewart Street, Suite 5220
Seattle, WA 98101-1271
(206) 553-7970

1 Although the City denies the existence of any pattern or practice of unconstitutional conduct by

2 SPD and its officers, it entered into the Agreement and Stipulated Order with the goal of

3 ensuring that SPD's policies, procedures, training, and oversight are sufficient to prevent

4 practices that the United States alleges contributed to a pattern or practice of constitutional

5 violations. The City also entered into the Agreements because it wishes to ensure that its police

6 department is functioning at an exceptional level and that it has positive relationships with all of

7 its communities.

8   17.   The Agreement and Stipulated Order's substantive provisions relate directly to the

9 policies, procedures, training, and oversight that the United States alleges contribute to a pattern

10 or practice of SPD officers using excessive force in violation of the Fourth Amendment and

11 Section 14141. For instance, the Agreement and Stipulated Order requires the City and SPD to

12 address policies and training related to: use of force, including use of impact weapons, escalation

13 of minor encounters, and force used against individuals with mental illness; discriminatory

14 policing; and front line and supervisory review of the use of force. The Agreement and

15 Stipulated Order also includes ongoing mechanisms to solicit input from SPD officers and

16 members of the Seattle community.

17   18.   Voluntary and mutually agreeable implementation of reforms is more likely to

18 conserve public resources and result in beneficial change than the uncertainties of litigation or an

19 order of this Court imposed at the end of protracted litigation.

20   19.   On July 31, 2012, the Court published on a publicly-accessible website notice of

21 the August 24, 2012 hearing to review the Joint Motion for Approval of the Settlement

22 Agreement and Stipulated Order of Resolution and Entry of Judgment and posted a copy of the

23

1   26.   The negotiations that culminated in the Agreement and Stipulated Order were

2   arms-length, not the product of fraud or overreaching by, or collusion between, the Parties. Such

3   negotiations underscore the reasonableness of the Agreement and Stipulated Order.

4   27.   There is an evidentiary basis for the Agreement and Stipulated Order, including

5   but not limited to the United States' investigation, and the input of many members of the

6   community.

7   28.   Through, in part, the Parties' extensive outreach to the City and its various diverse

8   communities, the Agreement and Stipulated Order is fair and adequately addresses the interests

9   of all concerned.

10   29.   "Because of the consensual nature of [such an agreement], voluntary compliance

11   is rendered more likely . . . . At the same time, the parties . . . minimize costly litigation and

12   adverse publicity and avoid the collateral effects of adjudicated guilt." *United States v. City of*

13   *Jackson, Miss.*, 519 F.2d 1147, 1152 n.9 (5th Cir. 1975). Indeed, "the value of voluntary

14   compliance is doubly important when it is a public employer that acts, both because of the

15   example its voluntary assumption of responsibility sets and because the remediation of

16   governmental discrimination is of unique importance." *Wygant v. Jackson Bd. of Educ.*, 476

17   U.S. 267, 290 (1986) (O'Connor, J., concurring).

18   30.   "Rule 52(c) provides the court may enter judgment after a party has been 'fully

19   heard.' ... The court was not required to receive live testimony." *Granite State Ins. Co. v. Smart*

20   *Modular Techs.*, 76 F.3d 1023, 1031 (9th Cir. 1996).

as modified by the parties' further stipulation and order entered this same day.

21   31.   In sum, entry of the Agreement and Stipulated Order is appropriate because, taken   *[initials]*

22   as a whole, the Agreement and Stipulated Order is fundamentally fair, adequate, and reasonable,

23   resulted from arms-length negotiations by sophisticated parties, is consistent with the purpose of

JOINT [PROPOSED] FINDINGS OF FACT AND CONCLUSIONS OF LAW - 9
12-CV-1282-JLRRBL

UNITED STATES ATTORNEY
700 Stewart Street, Suite 5220
Seattle, WA 98101-1271
(206) 553-7970

1   Section 14141, supported by an evidentiary record; and is the most effective way to address the

2   allegations of unconstitutional policing made by the United States.

3   32.   To the extent that any of the foregoing Findings of Fact are deemed to be

4   Conclusions of Law (or vice versa), they are incorporated into these Conclusions of Law (or vice

5   versa).

6   So stipulated and respectfully and jointly submitted on August 17, 2012.

7

8   For the UNITED STATES OF AMERICA:

     ERIC H. HOLDER, JR.
9   Attorney General of the United States of America

10
     JENNY A. DURKAN   THOMAS E. PEREZ
11   United States Attorney for the   Assistant Attorney General
     Western District of Washington   Civil Rights Division

12
     /s/ J. Michael Diaz   /s/ Timothy D. Mygatt
13   Kerry J. Keefe, Civil Chief   Jonathan M. Smith, Chief
     J. Michael Diaz, Assistant United States Attorney   Timothy D. Mygatt, Special Counsel
14   Rebecca S. Cohen, Assistant United States Attorney   Michelle L. Leung, Trial Attorney
     United States Attorney's Office   Michael J. Songer, Trial Attorney
15   Western District of Washington   United States Department of Justice
     700 Stewart Street, Suite 5220   Civil Rights Division- Special Lit. Section
16   Seattle, Washington 98101-1271   950 Pennsylvania Avenue, NW
     Phone: (206) 553-7970   Washington, DC 20530
17   Fax: (206) 553-4073   Phone: (202) 514-6255
     E-mail: Michael.Diaz@usdoj.gov   E-mail: Michelle.Leung@usdoj.gov

18
     For the CITY OF SEATTLE:

19
     PETER S. HOLMES
20   Seattle City Attorney

21   /s/ Peter S. Holmes
     PETER S. HOLMES, Seattle City Attorney
22   JEAN BOLER, Civil Chief
     SARAH K. MOREHEAD
23   Seattle City Attorney's Office
     PO Box 94769

JOINT [PROPOSED] FINDINGS OF FACT AND CONCLUSIONS OF LAW - 10
12-CV-1282-JLRRBL

UNITED STATES ATTORNEY
700 Stewart Street, Suite 5220
Seattle, WA 98101-1271
(206) 553-7970

122 | Wayne Perryman

[PROPOSED] ORDER APPROVING
THE JOINT FINDINGS OF FACT AND CONCLUSIONS OF LAW

AND NOW, this 21st day of Sept. , 2012, upon consideration of the foregoing, the Findings of Fact and Conclusions of Law are APPROVED and ENTERED in this *Preliminary approval* matter in the above-agreed form. ~~Approval~~ of the Settlement Agreement and ~~Entry of Judgment~~ *Stipulated Order of Resolution* shall be set out in a separate document. *modified*

_____
Hon. James L. Robart
United States District Court Judge

JOINT [PROPOSED] FINDINGS OF FACT AND CONCLUSIONS OF LAW - 12
12-CV-1282-JLRRBL.

UNITED STATES ATTORNEY
700 Stewart Street, Suite 5220
Seattle, WA 98101-1271
(206) 553-7970

U.S. Department of Justice

United States Attorney
Western District of Washington

Please reply to:
J. MICHAEL DIAZ
Assistant United States Attorney

700 Stewart Street, Suite 5220   Tel: (206) 553-7970
Seattle, Washington 98101-1271   Fax: (206) 553-4073
www.usdoj.gov/usao/waw

February 16, 2017

Via First Class U.S. Mail

Rev. Wayne Perryman
Humanity Diversity LLC
P.O. Box 256
Mercer Island, WA 98040
doublebro@aol.com

      Re: Your letter dated February 9, 2017

Dear Rev. Perryman,

      Thank you for your letter dated February 9, 2017, which we received on Tuesday, February 14.

      Even before receiving your letter, we also saw the statement by the Seattle Police Department (SPD) in the Seattle Post-Intelligencer (PI), which suggested that the United States Department of Justice (DOJ) or its United States Attorney's Office for the Western District of Washington (USAO) conducted an investigation or made a conclusion about whether or not there was any "bias or misconduct by any Seattle Police Officer involved in" the incident at issue in your lawsuit. That statement was not consistent with our civil jurisdiction in such matters or our internal processes, because, as I explained in my (re-attached) letters to you in 2015, we do not open a civil pattern and practice investigation of a police department based upon one complaint, however meritorious it may be. Consequently, again even before receiving your letter, we contacted the SPD, which agreed to correct its statement to delete any reference to the claim about the DOJ or USAO. Please see the attached story, which may also be found at the following website: http://www.seattlepi.com/local/crime/article/Lawsuit-SPD-wrongful-arrest-made-on-bias-10915691.php.

      Again, we appreciate the information you provided to the USAO. However, again, our jurisdiction is limited and we have no role is assessing the merits of individual claims in the civil law context.

      With that said, if you are still interested in having us testify in your trial, the law requires you to follow the DOJ's *Touhy* procedures, found at 28 C.F.R. Part 16.21 *et seq*., Subpart B.

//

Letter to Rev. Perryman
Page 2

Sincerely,

ANNETTE L. HAYES
United States Attorney

J. Michael Diaz

J. MICHAEL DIAZ
Assistant United States Attorney

Appendix 5

Mayor Jenny Durkan's Office Investigation of the Sean Perryman Case

From: doublebro <doublebro@aol.com>

To: jenny.durkan <jenny.durkan@seattle.gov>

Subject: The Sean Perryman Unjustified Arrest, By White Seattle Police Officers

Date: Sat, Jan 13, 2018 8:28 am

Dear Mayor Durkan

Sean Perryman, a black college student was arrested, charged with Third Degree Assault and jailed for four days because the Seattle Police chose not to look at one of the 16 surveillance cameras at the crime scene. Witnesses repeatedly pleaded with the police to look at the 11 second video before making the arrest, but the Seattle Police chose to listen to three false white witnesses instead, much like the white police during the Jim Crow era. The white witnesses were involved in the altercation. The police cams shows that the police chose not to interview other witnesses.

As soon as the Dan Satterberg seen the video, he dismissed the charges and apologized for the police's racist investigation. The video shows that it was a white security guard who attacked Sean's white friend and Sean intervened to stop the fight. When Sean's friend called the police and told the police that he wanted to press charges against the white man who assaulted him, the police ignored his request and chose to arrest Sean Perryman instead.

Sean's arrest record now shows up on many of the internet websites the specialize in background checks even though the case was dismissed because he never committed the crime that he was charged with. And all of this happened while the Seattle Police were operating under a Consent Decree of the Department of Justice.

The Black Community Is Angry & Want To Know:

1. Why did the Seattle Police refused to look at the surveillance video at the crime scene to determine who was telling the truth when witnesses asked them to do so?

2. Why did the Seattle Police have only three sworn witnesses, when there were several bystanders taking cell phone videos of the incident.

3 Why were the Seattle Police's three sworn witnesses the three white men who were the ones who attacked Sean Perryman and his friends and none of the other bystanders who witnessed the entire incident?

4. Why did the Police take 11 days before they decided to obtain a copy of the surveillance video? By then the video could have been taped over, erased or destroyed.

5. After viewing the video and learning that it was a white security guard, not Sean Perryman who started the altercation, why didn't the police drop the charges against Sean Perryman (who was merely acting in self-defense) and arrest the white security guard?

6. After learning that their three white witnesses had lied to get Sean Perryman arrested, why didn't the police charge those witnesses with *"lying to deceive a public*

official" which is a violation of Washington State Law?

7. Why did the investigating detective keep the video in his own personal possession and did not enter it as evidence until two weeks after the King County Prosecutor dismissed the case?

8. Why was there a double standard in this case. When the police thought that Sean Perryman had assaulted a white person, they arrested him immediately, but when they learned through watching the video, that it was the white security guard who initiated the assault and three white witnesses lied to cover up the assault, they refused to arrest and charge these individuals?

From: Nyland, Kelsey <Kelsey.Nyland@seattle.gov>
To: doublebro <doublebro@aol.com>
Subject: RE: Sean Perryman Case - 3 Days of Jail Hell - During Consent Decree
Date: Tue, Jan 16, 2018 11:17 am

Hi Rev. Perryman,

Yes – we did receive the packet. Thank you for sending that along!

Best,

Kelsey Nyland
Correspondence Assistant (She/Hers)
Mayor Jenny A. Durkan | City of Seattle
O: 206.684.5976 | kelsey.nyland@seattle.gov
Facebook | Twitter | Subscribe to Mayor Durkan's E-Newsletter

From: doublebro@aol.com [mailto:doublebro@aol.com]
Sent: Tuesday, January 16, 2018 10:35 AM
To: Nyland, Kelsey <Kelsey.Nyland@seattle.gov>
Subject: Re: Sean Perryman Case - 3 Days of Jail Hell - During Consent Decree

Thank you. We look forward to hearing from you. Did the Mayor get the package of information that I dropped off to her on Thursday? It had an autographed book in it and background information on Sean Perryman and myself Rev. Perryman.

Rev. Wayne perryman

-----Original Message-----
From: Nyland, Kelsey <Kelsey.Nyland@seattle.gov>
To: doublebro <doublebro@aol.com>
Sent: Tue, Jan 16, 2018 10:01 am
Subject: RE: Sean Perryman Case - 3 Days of Jail Hell - During Consent Decree

Dear Rev. Perryman,

Thank you for reaching out to Mayor Jenny Durkan regarding your son's experience with the SPD. I want to assure you that we are currently looking into this – you should expect to hear back from us by the end of this week.

Best,

Kelsey Nyland
Correspondence Assistant (She/Hers)
Mayor Jenny A. Durkan | City of Seattle
O: 206.684.5976 | kelsey.nyland@seattle.gov
Facebook | Twitter | Subscribe to Mayor Durkan's E-Newsletter

From: doublebro@aol.com [mailto:doublebro@aol.com]

-----Original Message-----
From: James Goods <james_goods@hotmail.com>
To: jenny.durkan <jenny.durkan@seattle.gov>
Sent: Sat, Jan 13, 2018 6:28 pm
Subject: Sean Perryman Case

Dear Mayor,

Respectfully ask that you to look in to Sean Perryman Case.

It's been some time since I've had the opportunity to review the details but had some initial concerns regarding the matrix of decisions and the timing of subsequent follow up investigation as well as evidence acquisition/review.

Although currently retired, formerly served as a law enforcement officer with two municipal agencies within King County.

Sincerely,

James Goods

Sent from my iPhone

       https://mail.aol.com/webmail-std/en-us/PrintMessage

From: Nyland, Kelsey <Kelsey.Nyland@seattle.gov>
To: 'dodblebro' <doublebro@aol.com>
Subject: RE: From Retired Police Officer: Sean Perryman Case
Date: Tue, Jan 30, 2018 1:52 pm

Hi Reverend Perryman,

I want to thank you again for your patience throughout this process, and I assure you that the Mayor's Office is currently reviewing your case, and that we have possession of the surveillance video you reference.

We've socialized your case throughout the Mayor's Office, and are struggling to find a path forward. While it is still under review, a formal communication is pending.

Sincerely,

Kelsey Nyland
Correspondence Assistant (She/Hers)
Mayor Jenny A. Durkan | City of Seattle
Facebook | Twitter | Subscribe to Mayor Durkan's E-Newsletter

From: doublebro@aol.com [mailto:doublebro@aol.com]
Sent: Tuesday, January 30, 2018 11:09 AM
To: Nyland, Kelsey <Kelsey.Nyland@seattle.gov>; lynsiburton@seattlepi.com; Durkan, Jenny <Jenny.Durkan@seattle.gov>; doublebro@aol.com
Subject: From Retired Police Officer: Sean Perryman Case

-----Original Message-----
From: James Goods <james_goods@hotmail.com>
To: jenny.durkan <jenny.durkan@seattle.gov>
Sent: Sat, Jan 13, 2018 6:28 pm
Subject: Sean Perryman Case

Dear Mayor,

Respectfully ask that you to look in to Sean Perryman Case.

It's been some time since I've had the opportunity to review the details but had some initial concerns regarding the matrix of decisions and the timing of subsequent follow up investigation as well as evidence acquisition/review.

Although currently retired, formerly served as a law enforcement officer with two municipal agencies within King County.

Sincerely,

James Goods

Appendix 6

Seattle Seahawks and Racial Discrimination

Remembering the Steelers Lowell Perry, the First African-American Coach in Modern NFL History

☐ Share Share with Steelers friends 16 Comments this Post 6 *is about a great All American Player who, in typical Steeler fashion back in the old days, suffered a career-ending injury before he finished his sixth game. BTSC interviewed Perry's widow, Maxine and his son, Lowell Perry Jr. Both wife and son expressed how grateful they were to the Rooney family. Perry was a young man in a strange town laying in a hospital for 13 weeks, his dreams of playing football shattered. Art Rooney made sure he wasn't a stranger for long.*

Lowell Perry was a college phenom. At the University of Michigan he played receiver and safety. He was an All-American who never left the field. The Steelers selected him in the eighth round of the 1953 NFL draft, a very high draft choice considering Perry was committed to the Air Force ROTC *for three years* before he would see a Steelers uniform.

The Steelers patience was finally rewarded in 1956. Lowell Perry was everything they hoped for and more. In just five-plus games he scored two touchdowns, including an electric 75-yard touchdown reception. He averaged an incredible 24 yards-per-reception and also racked up huge chunks of yardage returning punts and kickoffs. He even carried the ball twice for 37 yards. Unfortunately, one of those carries ended his playing career.

"It was a naked reverse against the Giants in the sixth game," lamented his son, Lowell Perry, Jr. "He was close to the sidelines when Rosey Grier, Dick Nolan and another guy all pounced on him. He landed on one of those steel yard markers."

True to his word, Rooney did offer more than just emotional support. When Perry was finally released from the hospital Rooney offered him a job. In 1957 Lowell W. Perry became the first African-American coach in modern NFL history. He coached the receivers. The next year Perry worked in the Steelers' scouting department. While employed by the Steelers, Perry went to law school at Duquesne University. He had great vision for a future outside of football. In 1966 Perry claimed another first when CBS hired him as a color analyst. He became the first African-American to broadcast an NFL game to a national audience.

Once a Steeler always a Steeler, even for less than six games. Perry went back to Pittsburgh for various alumni functions and took his son, Perry Jr., with him. On one of those trips Art Rooney invited Perry Jr. to work the 1973 training camp.

"That's the kind of guy he was," said Perry Jr. "He put me up in the dorm and let me eat with the players in the cafeteria. His sons, Dan and Artie, were just as nice. The warmth of the Rooney family is something I will never forget."

Perry Jr. had a summer vacation that would make any Steeler fan green with envy. He hung out with Mel Blount and Glen Edwards, played basketball with the guys and warmed up Terry Bradshaw on the sidelines. He was invited to team meetings and soaked it all in. Perry Jr. was entering his senior year in high school. He starred as a quarterback in football and also excelled in basketball and track.

"I remember Mr. Rooney introducing me to Joe Greene. He was bigger than life. When we shook hands his fingers ran halfway up my forearm. I decided right then and there I was going to play basketball in college," quipped Perry Jr.

Both Lowell Perrys went on to successful careers as public servants. Junior graduated from Yale, worked in the front office of the Seattle Seahawks for a decade and is now the chief executive officer of Big Brothers and Big Sisters of Middle Tennessee. Senior became the first African-American, another first, to run a major U.S. manufacturing facility when he worked for Chrysler in the 1970s. Senior chaired the Equal Employment Opportunities Commission under President Gerald Ford and was director of the Michigan Department of Labor. He was also a founding member of NFL Charities.

Maxine and Lowell had two more children who made their parents equally proud. Son Scott is currently the vice president of basketball operations for the Detroit Pistons and daughter Merrideth is an account manager for CennectEdu, an online college planning service to help high school students.

Lowell Perry Sr. (center) with Sons Scott (left) and Lowell Jr. (right)

"There's no doubt in my mind that Art Rooney had a profound affect on my father's life far beyond football," said Perry Jr. "Mr Rooney died in the house he lived most of his life in. The neighborhood completely changed color through the years, but Art Rooney never noticed."

His mother agrees. "Art Rooney did things for the neighbors that they never knew, like buy food and supplies and anything else that was needed. My husband was also a kind and caring individual whose outlook on life was definitely shaped by the Rooney family. And I can see it now in all three of our children."

Lowell Perry lost his bout with cancer in 2001, but not before leaving this world in better shape than he found it. The credo he gave his children is one we should all live by: "You make a living by what you earn, but you make a life by what you give." Thank you Lowell Perry.

Black Community Leader Saves Seahawks From
An Embarrassing Race Discrimination Law Suit

April 14, 2015

Attention:
Ed Goines, Seahawk General Counsel
John Schneider, Seahawk V.P & General Manager
Peter McLoughlin, Seahawk President/CEO

Gentlemen:

My name is Wayne Perryman, I am a die-hard Seahawk fan and I am also the black man who negotiated a settlement for the Seahawks preventing a very embarrassing race discrimination lawsuit during the tenure of Mike McCormick.

This letter is confidential and only intended to introduce you to myself and my son. It is not a shake-down letter nor is it blackmail, it is only intended to share with you the unfortunate experience that I had with former Seahawk owners Ken Berhing and Ken Hoffman while assisting them with a potentially explosive race discrimination lawsuit. The facts can be verified by Coach Chuck Knox, Gary Wright, Lowell Perry Jr. (son of the Pittsburg Steeler Lowell Perry Sr.), Seahawk minority owner, Ken Hoffman and unfortunately the late Mike McCormick who passed away.

Situation: Approximately six months before Mike McCormick accepted the job as president for the Carolina Panthers, I received a confidential phone call from Mike asking if I could help the Seahawks with a race related problem. At the time Lowell Perry Jr. was the Seahawks' Community Relations representative. Unfortunately, the Seahawks were receiving several complaints that Perry was not showing up at the events or showing up late. After several discussions with Perry with no improvements, Mike decided to let Perry go. Perry threatened to tell his dad who had a law degree, a lot of influence in the NFL and was the Federal Equal Employment Opportunity Commissioner under Gerald Ford. Mike called me because I was well known in the community and had an impressive track record of working with corporations in the area of race relations.

To make a long story short I negotiated a settlement and kept the situation from going public. Being thankful for my donated services, Mike asked if I would be interested in replacing Perry. Loving the Seahawks as I did and still do, I said yes. Mike was not only aware of my work in the community, he was also aware of my work with Seattle Mariner player Harold Reynolds and Seahawk player Curt Warner. Before hiring me, Mike had to get the approval of owner Ken Hoffman. Hoffman thanked me for helping them with the Perry situation and indicated that he thought I was the right man for the job. That is, until he learned that my wife was white. After meeting her, he declined his job offer. McCormick was angry.

After accepting the job with the Panthers, Mike asked if I would be interested in the same position with the new Carolina franchise. I gratefully turned him down. Today, my bi-racial son from that mixed marriage is 25, an honor student (on the Dean's List) at Central Washington University and he is trying to find either an internship or an opportunity with the Seahawks in some capacity. I am writing to request that if such an opportunity is available, would you please consider him (Sean Christian Perryman).

I know that you are **not** responsible for happened to me in the past under a different ownership and that you are not obligated in any way to try to right a wrong of the past. I just pray that you would give my son an opportunity to be a part of the same organization that once considered me as a viable candidate for a management position. Attached is a brief background on my son and what he has accomplished as a young man. We both attend the same church as Russell Wilson.

Blessings,

Wayne Perryman
P.O. Box 256
Mercer Island, WA 98040
(206) 708-6676

Appendix 7

NFL Forced Military to Pay NFL
$5.4 Million for Pre-game

Angry: Staff Sgt. Christopher Waiters, center, walks onto the field with fellow service members at MetLife Stadium during the New York Jets' Military Appreciation Game on Sunday

Payments: Military personnel salute before NFL game in what was seen as patriotic display before it was revealed the Department of Defense and National Guard paid clubs to appear

Proud: Medic Waiters gets a Distinguished Service Cross for his exceptionally valorous conduct while serving in Iraq. He said it was 'shameful' the US military was paying for them to appear at sports events

Outrage as NFL teams charge U.S. Defense Department $5.4MILLION in return for allowing troops to honor servicemen during football games

Soldier criticizes 'greedy' billionaire owners for taking payments

He spoke out after it was revealed NJ National Guard paid Jets $377,000

Military defended payments saying it is a useful recruitment tool

A US soldier has hit out against 'shameful' NFL teams cashing in on patriotic troop displays at sports games.

Army Staff Sgt. Christopher Waiters criticized the franchises after it was revealed the US Defense Department paid 14 NFL teams $5,4million to honor troops at games, over the last four years.

The army medic, who served on two tours of duty in Iraq and one in Afghanistan, blamed 'greed' of club owners.

Appendix 8
Government's Apologies for Slavery

Ш

109TH CONGRESS
1ST SESSION # S. RES. 39

Apologizing to the victims of lynching and the descendants of those victims
for the failure of the Senate to enact anti-lynching legislation.

IN THE SENATE OF THE UNITED STATES

FEBRUARY 7, 2005

Ms. LANDRIEU (for herself, Mr. ALLEN, Mr. LEVIN, Mr. FRIST, Mr. REID,
Mr. ALLARD, Mr. AKAKA, Mr. BROWNBACK, Mr. BAYH, Ms. COLLINS,
Mr. BIDEN, Mr. ENSIGN, Mrs. BOXER, Mr. HAGEL, Mr. CORZINE, Mr.
LUGAR, Mr. DAYTON, Mr. McCAIN, Mr. DODD, Ms. SNOWE, Mr. DUR-
BIN, Mr. SPECTER, Mr. FEINGOLD, Mr. STEVENS, Mrs. FEINSTEIN, Mr.
TALENT, Mr. HARKIN, Mr. JEFFORDS, Mr. JOHNSON, Mr. KENNEDY,
Mr. KOHL, Mr. LAUTENBERG, Mr. LEAHY, Mr. LIEBERMAN, Mr. NEL-
SON of Florida, Mr. PRYOR, and Mr. SCHUMER) submitted the following
resolution; which was referred to the Committee on the Judiciary

---

RESOLUTION

Apologizing to the victims of lynching and the descendants
of those victims for the failure of the Senate to enact
anti-lynching legislation.

Whereas the crime of lynching succeeded slavery as the ultimate expression of racism in the United States following
Reconstruction;

Whereas lynching was a widely acknowledged practice in the
United States until the middle of the 20th century;

2

Whereas lynching was a crime that occurred throughout the United States, with documented incidents in all but 4 States;

Whereas at least 4,742 people, predominantly African-Americans, were reported lynched in the United States between 1882 and 1968;

Whereas 99 percent of all perpetrators of lynching escaped from punishment by State or local officials;

Whereas lynching prompted African-Americans to form the National Association for the Advancement of Colored People (NAACP) and prompted members of B'nai B'rith to found the Anti-Defamation League;

Whereas nearly 200 anti-lynching bills were introduced in Congress during the first half of the 20th century;

Whereas, between 1890 and 1952, 7 Presidents petitioned Congress to end lynching;

Whereas, between 1920 and 1940, the House of Representatives passed 3 strong anti-lynching measures;

Whereas protection against lynching was the minimum and most basic of Federal responsibilities, and the Senate considered but failed to enact anti-lynching legislation despite repeated requests by civil rights groups, Presidents, and the House of Representatives to do so;

Whereas the recent publication of "Without Sanctuary: Lynching Photography in America" helped bring greater awareness and proper recognition of the victims of lynching;

Whereas only by coming to terms with history can the United States effectively champion human rights abroad; and

3

Whereas an apology offered in the spirit of true repentance moves the United States toward reconciliation and may become central to a new understanding, on which improved racial relations can be forged: Now, therefore, be it

1 *Resolved,* That the Senate—

2   (1) apologizes to the victims of lynching for the

3   failure of the Senate to enact anti-lynching legisla-

4   tion;

5   (2) expresses the deepest sympathies and most

6   solemn regrets of the Senate to the descendants of

7   victims of lynching, the ancestors of whom were de-

8   prived of life, human dignity, and the constitutional

9   protections accorded all citizens of the United

10   States; and

11   (3) remembers the history of lynching, to en-

12   sure that these tragedies will be neither forgotten

13   nor repeated.

○

IV

111TH CONGRESS
1ST SESSION **S. CON. RES. 26**

IN THE HOUSE OF REPRESENTATIVES

JUNE 18, 2009

Referred to the Committee on the Judiciary

CONCURRENT RESOLUTION

Apologizing for the enslavement and racial segregation of African-Americans.

Whereas during the history of the Nation, the United States has grown into a symbol of democracy and freedom around the world;

Whereas the legacy of African-Americans is interwoven with the very fabric of the democracy and freedom of the United States;

Whereas millions of Africans and their descendants were enslaved in the United States and the 13 American colonies from 1619 through 1865;

Whereas Africans forced into slavery were brutalized, humiliated, dehumanized, and subjected to the indignity of being stripped of their names and heritage;

Whereas many enslaved families were torn apart after family members were sold separately;

2

Whereas the system of slavery and the visceral racism against people of African descent upon which it depended became enmeshed in the social fabric of the United States;

Whereas slavery was not officially abolished until the ratification of the 13th amendment to the Constitution of the United States in 1865, after the end of the Civil War;

Whereas after emancipation from 246 years of slavery, African-Americans soon saw the fleeting political, social, and economic gains they made during Reconstruction eviscerated by virulent racism, lynchings, disenfranchisement, Black Codes, and racial segregation laws that imposed a rigid system of officially sanctioned racial segregation in virtually all areas of life;

Whereas the system of de jure racial segregation known as "Jim Crow", which arose in certain parts of the United States after the Civil War to create separate and unequal societies for Whites and African-Americans, was a direct result of the racism against people of African descent that was engendered by slavery;

Whereas the system of Jim Crow laws officially existed until the 1960s—a century after the official end of slavery in the United States—until Congress took action to end it, but the vestiges of Jim Crow continue to this day;

Whereas African-Americans continue to suffer from the consequences of slavery and Jim Crow laws—long after both systems were formally abolished—through enormous damage and loss, both tangible and intangible, including the loss of human dignity and liberty;

Whereas the story of the enslavement and de jure segregation of African-Americans and the dehumanizing atrocities committed against them should not be purged from or

SCON 26 RFH

3

minimized in the telling of the history of the United States;

Whereas those African-Americans who suffered under slavery and Jim Crow laws, and their descendants, exemplify the strength of the human character and provide a model of courage, commitment, and perseverance;

Whereas on July 8, 2003, during a trip to Goree Island, Senegal, a former slave port, President George W. Bush acknowledged the continuing legacy of slavery in life in the United States and the need to confront that legacy, when he stated that slavery "was . . . one of the greatest crimes of history . . . The racial bigotry fed by slavery did not end with slavery or with segregation. And many of the issues that still trouble America have roots in the bitter experience of other times. But however long the journey, our destiny is set: liberty and justice for all.";

Whereas President Bill Clinton also acknowledged the deep-seated problems caused by the continuing legacy of racism against African-Americans that began with slavery, when he initiated a national dialogue about race;

Whereas an apology for centuries of brutal dehumanization and injustices cannot erase the past, but confession of the wrongs committed and a formal apology to African-Americans will help bind the wounds of the Nation that are rooted in slavery and can speed racial healing and reconciliation and help the people of the United States understand the past and honor the history of all people of the United States;

Whereas the legislatures of the Commonwealth of Virginia and the States of Alabama, Florida, Maryland, and North Carolina have taken the lead in adopting resolu-

4

tions officially expressing appropriate remorse for slavery, and other State legislatures are considering similar resolutions; and

Whereas it is important for the people of the United States, who legally recognized slavery through the Constitution and the laws of the United States, to make a formal apology for slavery and for its successor, Jim Crow, so they can move forward and seek reconciliation, justice, and harmony for all people of the United States: Now, therefore, be it

1   *Resolved by the Senate (the House of Representatives*

2   *concurring),* That the sense of the Congress is the fol-

3   lowing:

4   (1) APOLOGY FOR THE ENSLAVEMENT AND

5   SEGREGATION OF AFRICAN-AMERICANS.—The Con-

6   gress—

7   (A) acknowledges the fundamental injus-

8   tice, cruelty, brutality, and inhumanity of slav-

9   ery and Jim Crow laws;

10   (B) apologizes to African-Americans on be-

11   half of the people of the United States, for the

12   wrongs committed against them and their an-

13   cestors who suffered under slavery and Jim

14   Crow laws; and

15   (C) expresses its recommitment to the

16   principle that all people are created equal and

17   endowed with inalienable rights to life, liberty,

5

1 and the pursuit of happiness, and calls on all
2 people of the United States to work toward
3 eliminating racial prejudices, injustices, and dis-
4 crimination from our society.
5 (2) DISCLAIMER.—Nothing in this resolution—
6   (A) authorizes or supports any claim
7 against the United States; or
8   (B) serves as a settlement of any claim
9 against the United States.

Passed the Senate June 18, 2009.

Attest: NANCY ERICKSON,
                                    Secretary.

CNN Politics.com

| HOME | WORLD | U.S. | POLITICS | CRIME | ENTERTAINMENT | HEALTH | TECH | TRAVEL | LIVING | BUSINESS | SPOR |

Hot Topics ♪ Election Center • Political Ticker • Commentary • Obama • McCain • Electoral map • more topics ♦

Set your CNN.com Edition ◉ CNN U.S. ○ CNN Internatio

House apologizes for slavery, 'Jim Crow' injustices

WASHINGTON (CNN) -- The House of Representatives on Tuesday passed a resolution apologizing to African-Americans for slavery and the era of Jim Crow.

The House on Tuesday evening passed a resolution apologizing for slavery and Jim Crow laws.

The nonbinding resolution, which passed on a voice vote, was introduced by Rep. Steve Cohen, a white lawmaker who represents a majority black district in Memphis, Tennessee.

While many states have apologized for slavery, it is the first time a branch of the federal government has done so, an aide to Cohen said.

In passing the resolution, the House also acknowledged the "injustice, cruelty, brutality and inhumanity of slavery and Jim Crow."

"Jim Crow," or Jim Crow laws, were state and local laws enacted mostly in the Southern and border states of the United States between the 1870s and 1965, when African-Americans were denied the right to vote and other civil liberties and were legally segregated from whites.

The name "Jim Crow" came from a character played by T.D. "Daddy" Rice who portrayed a slave while in blackface during the mid-1800s.

The resolution states that "the vestiges of Jim Crow continue to this day."

"African-Americans continue to suffer from the consequences of slavery and Jim Crow -- long after both systems were formally abolished -- through enormous damage and loss, both tangible and intangible, including the loss of human dignity and liberty, the frustration of careers and professional lives, and the long-term loss of income and opportunity," the resolution states.

The House also committed itself to stopping "the occurrence of human rights violations in the future."

Don't Miss

- In Depth: 'Black In America'
- IReport.com: Your take on 'Black in America'

The resolution does not address the controversial issue of reparations. Some members of the African-American community have called on lawmakers to give cash payments or other financial benefits to descendents of slaves as compensation for the suffering caused by slavery.

It is not the first time lawmakers have apologized to an ethnic group for injustices.

In April, the Senate passed a resolution sponsored by Sen. Sam Brownback, R-Kansas, that apologized to Native Americans for "the many instances of violence, maltreatment and neglect."

In 1993 the Senate also passed a resolution apologizing for the "illegal overthrow" of the Kingdom of Hawaii in 1893.

In 1988, Congress passed and President Reagan signed an act apologizing to the 120,000 Japanese-

US Senate votes formal apology for slavery

By Olivier Knox – Jun 18, 2009

WASHINGTON (AFP) — The US Senate approved a fiercely worded resolution Thursday formally apologizing for the "fundamental injustice, cruelty, brutality, and inhumanity of slavery" of African-Americans.

The unanimous voice vote came five months after Barack Obama became the first black US president, and ahead of the June 19 "Juneteenth" celebration of the emancipation of African-Americans at the end of the US Civil War in 1865.

House of Representatives approval, which could come as early as next week, would make it the first time the entire US Congress has formally apologized on behalf of the American people for one of the grimmest wrongs in US history.

The bill, which does not require Obama's signature, states that the US Congress "acknowledges the fundamental injustice, cruelty, brutality, and inhumanity of slavery and Jim Crow laws" that enshrined racial segregation at the state and local level in the United States well into the 1960s.

And the Congress "apologizes to African-Americans on behalf of the people of the United States, for the wrongs committed against them and their ancestors who suffered under slavery and Jim Crow laws."

It also recommits lawmakers "to the principle that all people are created equal and endowed with inalienable rights to life, liberty, and the pursuit of happiness, and calls on all people of the United States to work toward eliminating racial prejudices, injustices, and discrimination from our society."

Democratic Senator Tom Harkin of Iowa and Republican Sam Brownback of Kansas led the debate as both major US parties banished their deep differences on subjects like the economy to come together on the measure.

"We pledge to move beyond this shameful period and we officially acknowledge and apologize for the institution of slavery in this country what many refer to as 'the original sin of America,'" said Brownback.

"Let us make no mistake: This resolution will not fix lingering injustices. while we are proud of this resolution and believe it is long overdue, the real work lies ahead," said Harkin.

In a step that has angered some African-American lawmakers, the measure takes pains not to fuel the push for the US government to pay reparations to the descendants of African slaves.

"Nothing in this resolution (a) authorizes or supports any claim against the United States; or (b) serves as a settlement of any claim against the United States," it says.

That has drawn "serious concerns" within the Congressional Black Caucus, though the group has yet to decide on a formal position towards the legislation, a source close to the group said Thursday.

It was unclear whether opposition from those lawmakers could force a change to the language or otherwise hinder the measure.

And Harkin said a "fitting ceremony" to mark final passage would occur in early July. Supporters hope Obama will attend the event.

Former president Bill Clinton expressed regret for slavery during a March 1998 trip to Africa, while his successor, George W. Bush, called slavery "one of the greatest crimes of history" during a July 2003 visit to Goree Island, Senegal, a former slave-trade port.

Some US states have officially adopted resolutions expressing regret or remorse for slavery.

Appendix 9
Lebron James, Carmelo Anthony, Chris Paul, and Dwayne Wade's ESPY Awards

LeBron James, Dwyane Wade, Carmelo Anthony and Chris Paul Deliver Powerful Black Lives Matter Opening Speech at ESPYs

Kevin Winter/Getty Images

ROSE MINUTAGLIO July 13, 2016 09:25 PM

[BRIGHTCOVE "21018438" "" "peoplenow" "auto"]The 2016 ESPY Awards opened with a powerful Black Lives Matter message from four of the biggest names in the NBA.

Carmelo Anthony, Chris Paul, Dwyane Wade and LeBron James took the stage on Wednesday to spread a message of love and acceptance during a week riddled with gun violence and fear – including the shooting of 12 police officers at a Dallas Black Lives Matter march and the deaths of Alton Sterling and Philando Castile.

Anthony, a forward on the New York Knicks, opened with a statement on behalf of Paul, Wade and James.

"The four of us we cannot ignore the realities of the current state of America," he said. "The events of the past week have put a spotlight on the injustice, distrust and anger that plague so many of us. The system is broken. But the problems are not new, the violence is not new and the racial divide definitely is not new."

He adds, "But the urgency for change is at an all time high."

Wade of the Miami Heat begged for racial profiling to end.

"Not seeing the value of black and brown bodies has to stop but also the retaliation has to stop. The needless gun violence in places like Chicago, Dallas, not to mention Orlando it has to stop, enough. Enough is enough," the basketball star said. "Now as athletes it's on us to challenge each other to do even more than we already do in our own communities. The conversation cannot stop as our schedules get busy again. It wont always be convenient, it won't. It won't always be comfortable but it is necessary."

James, Wade's former teammate on the Heat and a current free-agent, argued that feeling "helpless and frustrated by the violence" is not acceptable. And he used his time on stage to ask viewers to consider a call to action.

"It's time to look in the mirror and ask ourselves what are we doing to create change I know tonight we are honoring Muhammad Ali,l the 'G.O.A.T.' but to do his legacy any justice let's use this moment as a call to action for all professional athlete to educate ourselves, explore these issues, speak up, use our influence and renounce all violence. And most importantly go back to our communities, invest our time, our resources, help rebuild them help strengthen them help change them," James, born in Akron, Ohio, said. "We all have to do better."

And Paul, a guard for the Los Angeles Clippers, says he has a nephew who is a police officer.

"[My nephew] is one of the hundreds of thousands of great officers serving this country. But Trayvon Martin, Michael Brown, Tamir Rice, Eric Garner, Laquan McDonald, Alton Sterling, Philando Castile.. this is also our reality," he says, naming the victims of brutal shootings. "Generations ago, legends like Jesse Owens, Jackie Robinson, Muhammad Ali, John Carlos and Tommy smith. Abdul-Karim al-Jabbar, Jim Brown Billie Jean King, Arthur Ashe and countless others They set a model for what athletes should stand for. So we choose to stand in their footsteps."

Appendix 10
List of Abolitionists

Abolitionist & Underground Railroad
Study By Rev. Wayne Perryman

Thaddeus Stevens	Attorney/Congressman	Un - 282
Salmon P. Chase	Attorney	Un – 282
William H. Seward	Attorney	Un – 282
Rutherford B. Hayes	Attorney/President	Un – 282
Jon Jolliffe	Attorney	Un – 282
Albert G. Riddle	Attorney	Un – 282
Rufus P. Spalding	Attorney	Un – 282
Rush R. Sloane	Attorney	Un – 281
Josiah Quincy	Attorney/Harvard Pres	Un – 283
Richard H. Dana	Attorney	Un – 283
Robert Rantoul Jr.	Attorney	Un – 283
Ellis Gray Loring	Attorney	Un – 283
Samuel E. Swell	Attorney	Un – 283
Charles G. Davis	Attorney	Un – 283
James H. Collins	Attorney	Un – 283
John M. Wilson	Attorney	Un - 283
E.S. Leland	Attorney/Judge	Un- 283
B.C. Cook	Attorney	Un – 283
O.C. Gray	Attorney	Un – 284

J.O. Glover	Attorney	Un – 284
Isaac N. Arnold	Attorney	Un – 284
Joseph Knox	Attorney	Un – 284
J. V. Eustace	Attorney	Un – 284
E.C. Larnard	Attorney	Un – 284
James Vincent	Attorney	Un – 284
Lewis Mason	Attorney	Un – 284
David Paul Brown	Attorney	Un – 284
William S. Pierce	Attorney	Un – 285
John Dean	Attorney	Un – 285
Judge Mellen Chamberlain	Judge	Un – 36
Judge Jabez Wright	Judge	Un - 39
Judge Thomas Lee	Judge	Un – 58
Judge Thomas Mitchell	Judge	Un – 58
Judge William Sowles	Judge	Un – 107
Judge John West	Judge	Un – 107
Judges Joseph Poland	Judge	Un – 107
Judge A.J. Russell	Judge	Un – 107
Judge Joseph Poland	Judge	Un - 130
Con. Joshua Giddings	Congressman	Un – 63, 105
Con. James M. Ashley	Congressman	Un - 92

Con. Thaddeus Stevens	Congressman	Un – 106
Con. Sidney Edgerton	Congressman	Un – 106
Sen. Jacob M. Howard	Senator	Un - 106
Sen. Lawrence Brainerd	Senator	Un – 107
Sen. Charles Sumner	Senator	Un - 173
Con. Josiah B. Grinnell	Congressman	Un - 108
Rev. Alvah Sabin	Clergy/Congressman	Un - 107
Rev. Samuel J. May	Clergy	Un – 36
Rev. O.B. Cheney	Clergy/College Pres	Un – 37
Rev. James Gilliland	Clergy	Un - 41
Rev. John Rankin	Clergy	Un – 53, 63, 96
Rev. John Cross	Clergy	Un – 50
Rev. John B. Mahan	Clergy	Un – 53
Rev. Charles T. Torrey	Clergy	Un - 28
Rev. J. Porter	Clergy	Un - 63
Rev. Calvin Fairbanks	Clergy	Un – 65
Rev. Samuel J. May	Clergy	Un – 105
Rev. Own Lovejoy	Clergy	Un - 107
Rev. John B. Mahan	Clergy	Un - 150
Rev. Asa Turner	Clergy	Un – 114
Rev. Thomas Clement	Clergy	Un – 123

Rev. Charles Ray	Clergy	Un – 126
Rev. Joshua Young	Clergy	Un - 130
Rev. Samuel J. May	Clergy	Un – 131
Rev. Theodore Parker	Clergy	Un - 180
Dr. Isaac B. Beck	Doctor	Un – 53
Dr. Alexander Campbell	Doctor	Un – 53
Dr. Alexander Ross	Doctor	Un – 28-30 104-183
Dr. Bailey	Doctor	Un – 64
Dr. Nathan M. Thomas	Doctor	Un – 88
Dr. J.A. Bingham	Doctor	Un - 89
Dr. Norton S. Townshend	Doctor	Un – 104
Dr. Jared P. Kirtland	Doctor	Un - 104
General Reed	Ship Owner	Un – 82
Captain Appleby	Ship Captain	Un – 82
Captain Steele	Ship Captain	Un – 82
Captain Kelsey	Ship Captain	Un – 82
Captain A.P. Dutton	Ship Captain	Un – 82
Captain John G. Weiblen	Ship Captain	Un – 83
Col. James Kilbourne	Officer	Un - 84
Col. John Stone	Officer	Un – 56
General McIntire	Officer	Un – 88

Col. Thomas W. Higginson	Officer	Un – 105
Gen. Samuel Fessenden	Officer	Un – 106
Gen. Samuel Fessenden	Officer	Un - 133
Col. Johnathan P Miller	Officer	Un – 106
✳ **Gerritt Smith**	Wealthy Philanthropist	Un - 107
Isaac T. Hooper	Store Owner	Un – 34
Lewis Tappan	Rich Store Owner	Un – 180
Arthur Tappan	Rich Store Owner	Let – 46 70-87
Joseph Garretson	Merchant	Un - 57
Edward Orton	Professor	Un – 35
Levi Coffin	Banker	Un – 40 Let 78
Jervis Langdon	Prominent Citizen	Un - 128
Thurlow Weed	Media/journalist	Un – 108
Syndney Howard Gay	Media/Editor	Un – 108
Mr. Poindexter	Barber	Un - 151
William Lloyd Garrison	Quaker	Un - 303-308
Hannah Gibbons	Wife	Let - 36
George W.S. Lucas	**Negro**	Un – 70
George L. Burroughes	**Negro**	Un – 70
Stephens Meyers	**Negro**	Un – 70
George De Baptist	**Negro**	Un – 70

George Dolarson	**Negro**	Un – 70
Gabe N. Johnson	**Negro**	Un – 64
Rev. W.M. Mitchell	**Clergy/Negro**	Un – 45
Frederick Douglass	**Negro**	Un – 35
Harriet Tubman	**Negro**	Un – 6, 178, 185
John H. Stewart	**Negro**	Un - 89
William H. Merritt	**Negro**	Un – 92
Wash Spradley	**Negro**	Un – 150
John Mason	**Negro**	Un - 184
J.R. Ware	Unknown	Un – 69
Levi Rathbun	Unknown	Un – 69
Peter Stewart	Unknown	Un - 69
Vestal Coffin	Unknown	Un – 40
Addison Coffin	Unknown	Un - 40
Frederick Nicholson	Unknown	Un - 35
Brown Thurston	Unknown	Un – 37
John Sloane	Unknown	Un – 37
David Hudson	Unknown	Un – 37
John Leeper	Unknown	Un - 41
Own Brown	Father of John Brown	Un – 37
Edward Howard	Unknown	Un – 37

Abby Kelly	Unknown	Un – 49
William Steel	Unknown	Un – 51
David Putnam	Unknown	Un – 51
Point Harmar	Unknown	Un - 51
Amos Pettijohn	Unknown	Un – 53
William McCoy	Unknown	Un – 53
John Charles	Unknown	Un – 53
G.W. Weston	Unknown	Un - 58
Abram Allen	Unknown	Un – 59
Calvin Fairbank	Unknown	Un – 61
James W. Torrence	Unknown	Un – 61
William I. Bowditch	Unknown	Un - 61
James Westwater	Unknown	Un – 63
Eli F. Brown	Unknown	Un – 64
Edward Hardwood	Unknown	Un – 64
W.H. Brisbane	Unknown	Un – 64
John Fairbanks	Unknown	Un – 65
Sidney Speed	Unknown	Un - 65
Anthony Bingey	Unknown	Un – 76
Aaron L. Benedict	Unknown	Un – 76
Wells Brown	Unknown	Un – 77

William Still	Unknown	Un – 77
Elijah F. Pennypacker*	Unknown	Un – 88
Philo Carpenter*	Unknown	Un - 88
H.B. Leeper*	Unknown	Un – 88
Leverett B. Hill*	Unknown	Un – 88
Van Dorn*	Unknown	Un – 88
W.D. Schooley*	Unknown	Un – 88
Johnathan H. Gray*	Unknown	Un – 88
Milton Hill*	Unknown	Un – 88
John H. Frazee*	Unknown	Un – 88
Ozem Gardner*	Unknown	Un – 89
George J. Payne	Unknown	Un – 89
Thomas L. Gray	Unknown	Un – 89
Theodore Parker	Unknown	Un – 90
Richard Mott	Unknown	Un – 92
James Conlisk	Unknown	Un – 92
Lyman Goodnow	Unknown	Un – 92
John Van Zandt	Unknown	Un – 102
Daniel Kauffman	Unknown	Un – 102
Wendell Phillips	Unknown	Un -103
T.W. Higginson	Unknown	Un – 103

Ellis Gray Loring	Unknown	Un -103
Samuel Cabot Jr.	Unknown	Un – 103
Henry J. Prentiss	Unknown	Un – 103
John A. Andrew	Unknown	Un – 103
Samuel G. Howe	Unknown	Un – 103
James Freeman Clarke	Unknown	Un – 103
Richard j. Hinton	Unknown	Un - 114
John Hunn	Unknown	Un – 117
Ezekiel Hunn	Unknown	Un – 117
Jacob Biglow	Unknown	Un -117
Elijah Pennypacker	Unknown	Un – 121
Cornelius Cornell	Unknown	Un – 124
John Everett	Unknown	Un – 124
Eber M. Pettit	Unknown	Un – 125
Mr. T.	Unknown	Un -125
David Ruggles	Unknown	Un – 126
Stephen Meyers	Unknown	Un – 126
Mr. Gibbs	Unknown	Un – 126
J.W. Loguen	Unknown	Un – 126
Hiram Wilson	Unknown	Un – 126
Mr. Martin I. Townsend	Unknown	Un - 126

Philo Carpenter	Unknown	Un - 147
Nathaniel P. Borden	Unknown	Un – 130
Robert Adams	Unknown	Un – 130
Mr. & Mrs. Chace	Unknown	Un – 130
Rowland E. Robinson	Unknown	Un - 130
Jethro & Anne Mitchell	Unknown	Un – 131
Daniel Mitchell	Unknown	Un – 131
Effingham L. Capron	Unknown	Un – 131
William I. Bowditch	Unknown	Un – 132
William Jackson	Unknown	Un – 132
Stephen & Abby Foster	Unknown	Un – 132
Mary E. Crocker	Unknown	Un – 132
James Furber	Unknown	Un – 133
S.T. Pickard	Unknown	Un – 133
Oliver Dennett	Unknown	Un – 133
Nathan Winslow	Unknown	Un – 133
Brown Thurston	Unknown	Un – 133
Thomas Williams	Unknown	Un – 136
I. Newton Peirce	Unknown	Un -143
George Fox	Quaker Leader	Un - 93
Germans Abolitionist	Unknown	Un - 92

Thomas Garrett	Farmer	Un – 53
Horace Holt	Farmer	Un – 60
Deacon Jirch Platt	Farmer	Un – 63
Hannah Marsh	Farmer/wife	Un- 50, 60
Joseph Sider	Peddler	Un - 60

References

# Underground Participants	Page 87
Number of Slaves Helped	Page 87-89,
Political Parties	Page 97, 99-100
Transport by Water	Pages 81-83, 143-149
Church Involvement	Pages 93-97
Number of Slaves Escaped	Page 341
Tubman v John Mason	Page 184, 186

A Narrative Biography
of Wayne Perryman

Remembering what it was like to grow up in a broken home, often times with no food, and no toys for Christmas and seemly no hope for a better life, Rev. Wayne Perryman made a commitment to do everything he could to help the poor and the under-privileged. In 1967, his efforts to feed the poor were discovered by Lane Smith, the Religion Editor for the Seattle Times. Smith publicized Perryman's work in a front-page featured story of the Seattle Times on December 8, 1967. The headlines read: Payoff on a Dream: Hungry Kids Gain a Helper."

Being self-reliant, Perryman started his own non-profit organization (Operation Destitution) and financed his charitable projects through number of benefit concerts, featuring his own group: *"The Gospel O.D. Singers"* (O.D. for Operation Destitution). In 1972, the group released its first hit first record album and used the royalties to fund their projects. Over the years, the gospel group raised thousands of dollars to feed the poor, provide clothes and toys for needy children and donated equipment and supplies to a multitude of community-based organizations that catered to the needs of those who were less fortunate. During the life of Perryman's organization, Perryman never received a salary, nor did his organization ever request funds from a government agency.

One of the recipients of Operation Destitution, was a program called Sea-Dru-Nar (Seattle Drug and Narcotic), the Pacific Northwest's first drug rehabilitation center. The program was started by Jerry Sanders, a three-time convicted felon and ex-drug addict. Jerry not only needed funding and equipment for this new program, he also needed someone to care for his two young daughters whose mother had died of an overdose. Since the live-in facility was no place to raise two girls, Perryman and his wife applied for a Washington State Foster Care License and took the girls into their home. Years later after Sanders left Sea-Dru-Nar he started a new program called: the Conquest House.

Perryman & Inner-city Gangs

Prior to Operation Destitution, Perryman coached sports for Seattle's Parks Department and for the Rotary Boys Club. The boys club was built in the heart of inner-city by the Seattle chapter of Rotary International. His work with young men expanded when he negotiated a truce between two rival gangs in 1989. Perryman's commitment to young men was well-known and he had won the trust and respect of local gang leaders. When he approached the rival leaders regarding a possible truce, they agreed on two conditions: (1) that he provide a secure and secret location for the meeting and (2) that he bring together black leaders in the African

American community so they could voice their concerns. Attending the meeting were Washington State Representative, Jessie Wineberry; Councilman Norm Rice, who became Seattle's first black mayor; King County Councilman, Ron Sims, who became the County's first black Executive; Seattle School Board member, Michael Preston and the former star running-back for the University of Washington, State Senator, George Fleming (Fleming was recently inducted into the Rose Bowl Hall of Fame in 2012). Only one reporter was allowed to attend the meeting - Alex Tizon of the Seattle Times. Through this meeting, chaired by Perryman, a truce was agreed to and gang violence in Seattle reduced drastically. One year later, when California gangs ("Crips" & "Bloods") plotted major warfare against Seattle's "Black Gangster Disciples" (in an effort to expand their territory in Washington State), gang leaders contacted Perryman. Perryman, supported by the community's top black leaders, called an emergency meeting with Seattle's Police Chief, Patrick Fitzsimons and Mayor Charles Royer. After the plot was verified by the Los Angeles Police's Gang Unit, every off-duty Seattle police officer was ordered back to work immediately. When the gangs gathered at the planned location, they were shocked to find a massive police presence. The crowd was disbursed without incident. As their lifestyle changed, gang members voluntarily surrendered to Perryman a variety of weapons, including an AK-47. The weapons were turned over to authorities. When ex-gang members needed someone to appear in court on their behalf, Perryman was there, and when they needed money to purchase books for college, it was Perryman, not the politician who came through for them.

Motivational High School Assemblies

With start-up funds from Kelly Waller, President of SAFECO Insurance, and Phil Smart Sr. of Phil Smart Mercedes Dealerships, Perryman's work with gangs and "at-risk" youth moved to the next level when he co-founded a new gang prevention program called: "Youth Challenge." The new program sponsored motivational assemblies for high schools, using star players from the Seattle Seahawk's (NFL), (former) Dallas Cowboys, Seattle Sonics and the Seattle Mariners (MBL). Youth Challenge outfitted the players with professional basketball uniforms and scheduled them to play teams from local high schools. After the exhibition game, the celebrity players shared their personal testimonies and explained how they overcame the temptations of gangs and drugs while growing up in the inner city and in the rural communities of America. The success of this program paved the way for a series of new innovative character-building classes developed by Perryman and his volunteer staff. An entire student body from one high school was required to take his classes on Peer Pressure, Race Relations and the power of Positive Role Models (the school provided the classrooms). The program was so successful, that students from another inner city high school dedicated an entire page in their high school year-book to honor the program. No government funds were used or requested for this program and Perryman received no salary.

Role Models for Inner-city Youth

Through Perryman's work, he realized that although his programs were very effective, they lacked one key ingredient, positive role models. To fill this need he formed, Role Models Unlimited. To recruit positive black male role models, Perryman turned to his friend and colleague, all-star second basemen, Harold Reynolds of the Seattle Mariners. On January 14, 1990, Perryman and Reynolds sponsored **"The Back Home Banquet for Brothers."** The black-tie event was attended by over 2,000 black men from all walks of life which included everyone from college professors to players and coaches of the Seattle Seahawks (NFL), the Seattle Mariners (MLB), and Seattle's, Super-Sonics (NBA). With performances by "Grammy Award Winner" Carvin Winans, the event caught the attention of the national media including USA Today and Sports Illustrated magazine. The week following the banquet (as planned), hundreds of black men filled the inner-city schools and invited the students to be their guest for lunch. Students from single-parent homes were shocked to see the hundreds of black men that filled the halls and lunch rooms of their schools and many became friends for a lifetime. Those who participated in the program said it changed their lives forever. Other states requested information to start similar programs. Role Models Unlimited received no money from the government and Perryman received no salary.

Perryman & Children's Foundation

Impressed by Perryman's commitment to young people along with his own personal desire to become more involved in the community, Harold Reynolds asked Perryman to help him establish the Harold Reynolds's Children Foundation. Through Perryman's creative leadership, the foundation produced character-building storybooks for small children (featuring Ken Griffrey Jr. and other Mariner stars); it provided food and funds for winter utility bills for the poor, and financed an entire inner-city Little League, consisting of 13 teams. Because of this work, Harold was invited to the Whitehouse and honored by President George H. Bush as a recipient of Bush's Points of Light Award; he received the Martin Luther King Humanitarian Award and baseball's prestigious Roberto Clemente Award.

4

The children's books, authored by Wayne Perryman, were the first children's book to be placed in the Baseball Hall of Fame Library on October 19, 1989. Ten thousand books were given to children during a Mariner's baseball game and thousands of others were donate to children in the Seattle Public Schools. A similar children's book was developed for Chuck Knox, coach of the Seattle Seahawks and it was placed in the Pro-Football Hall of Fame on the same day (October 19, 1989).

Perryman's Work with U.S. Senators & Schools

During his tenure as U.S. Senator, Senator Slade Gorton issued a Congressional Resolution to honor Wayne Perryman and asked him serve on the Senator's advisory board for gang activity. Shortly after, the Puget Sound Educational Service District, asked Perryman to join their staff, specifically to develop anti-gang educational programs for the 500 schools and the 300,000 students in their district as the Director of the Regional Educational Alliance on Gang Activity. During that year, Perryman authored one of the nation's first books on gangs for teachers, school administrators and law enforcement officers; he partnered with KOMO T.V. (an ABC affiliate) and produced a film documentary on gangs and conducted several training sessions for principals and school officials. In addition to working with Senator Gorton, he established relationships with Ms Donna Brazile, chairwoman of the Democratic National Committee and advised Reince Priebus, the Chairman of the Republican National Committee regarding outreach to the black community. Priebus later became the Chief of Staff for President Donald Trump.

Providing A Safe Place for Teens

In 1997, to provide a safe place for "at-risk" youth, Perryman partnered with his church to transform an old building into a modern-day teen center. Working 14 hour days (without pay), he devoted the entire summer of 1997 to the project and completed it in time for the fall season. The center was equipped with a big-screen TV, a surround-sound stereo system, a stage for performing arts, a video game room, a computer room for studies, a kitchen for food service, an outdoor picnic area for barbecues, and an outdoor basketball and sports court equipped with lights for night time activities (later, they added equipment to record music). When the project was completed, over 800 youth attended the grand-opening and the Seattle Times' article read: Miracle on 23rd Ave." No government funds were used on this project and Perryman received no salary.

5

Serving On Committees & Boards

Although Rev. Perryman spent a considerable amount of time on his own projects, he always had time to assist other organizations. He served on the Advisory Board for Seattle Central Community College, he was chairman of the Seattle Public Schools' Occupational Educational Steering Committee, member of the National Council on Crime and Delinquency, National Program Director for "Brothers," served as Loaned Executive for the United Way, member of the Seattle Coalition for Clergy, and for 30 years, he continued to coach sports (both boys' and girls'). When the Mercer Island Youth and Family Services needed someone to head-up their fund-raiser, Perryman was selected as the chair. He proposed a community project similar to the "Guinness Book of Records," followed by a celebrity basketball game. Perryman took the lead and set a record by baking a 37 feet chocolate cake. The month-long activity of setting records was followed by the celebrity basketball game, featuring quarterback Jim Zorn of the Seattle Seahawks and NFL Hall of Fame wide-receiver, Steve Largent. The capacity-filled gym produced several thousand dollars for the youth agency. Pieces of the 37 foot chocolate cake were auctioned off during half time. At the end of half time, only the crumbs were left.

Professional Experience

Perryman's employment tenure include working for three separate billion dollar corporations managing Human Resources and Labor Relations for Todd Shipyard Corporation, Ingersoll-Rand and RCA. His professional career also included providing Employment Relations consulting services for government agencies and many of our nation's Fortune 500 companies. His client list included Honeywell, Nordstrom Stores, the Boeing Company, Continental Can, West Coast Grocers, The Bon (now Macy's Department Store), and the Department of Defense along with a multitude of city and county governments, police departments and school districts.

Legal Assistance for the Poor

With a corporate background in fact-finding investigations, employment relations and employment law, Perryman used these skills to assist victims of discrimination who could not afford an attorney and/or those who were denied legal representation by the NAACP, Urban League and other community-based organizations. While representing women, African Americans, Latinos, Asians and men over 40, Perryman only lost one case in 30 years. His cases involving the

Longshore industry resulted in a settlement of over three million dollars. On Sunday March 23, 1997, the Seattle Times published a three page article featuring the landmark case. From Labor & Industries cases to discrimination cases and cases involving Veteran benefits, Perryman successfully negotiated settlements on behalf of his friends and clients without charge, including quietly negotiating a racial discrimination settlement for the Seattle Seahawks at the request of President and General Manager, Mike McCormack and minority owner Ken Hoffman (the Lowell Perry Jr. case).

Equal Opportunity Assistance

To assist companies with their Affirmative Action needs, Perryman partnered with major corporations and produced a career recruiting book for schools, colleges and community organizations. The book was designed to provide ethnic minorities and women with the job requirements needed to qualify for employment. Companies involved with the "Affirmative Action Career Communicator" publication (as it was called), included the Boeing Company, Honeywell, Pacific Northwest Bell, Western International Hotels, Todd Shipyards, Lockheed, Sundstrand Data Control, SAFECO Corporation, and the John Fluke to name a few. To further assist corporations with employment issues, Perryman produced a five volume 220 minute (VHS) video series entitled: "Preventing Litigation in the Workplace" in addition to publishing the Northwest Employment Journal, America's first Employment Relations quarterly newspaper. The publication featured articles from experts (and politicians) on employment-related issues. Guest editorialist included Senator Edward Kennedy, the Rev. Jesse Jackson, Congressman Mike Lowery, the Reagan Administration and corporate executives. Further assistance was provided for companies having difficulty finding ethnic minorities models for their advertising campaigns. To meet this need, Perryman started Topaz Modeling Agency, the only modeling agency on the west coast that provided models of color for many department stores in the Pacific Northwest including Nordstrom Stores. Perryman received no fee for representing his models and paid for all of the model's expenses. The modeling agency became a featured story in the Fashion section of the Seattle Times on August 12, 1976.

Wayne Perryman Talk Show Host

In 1973, Perryman hosted "Wayne Perryman Show" on KTW in Seattle. The prime time weekend talk show featured prominent guests and movies stars from around the country. Following the "Wayne Perryman Show," was the station's sports show, featuring former Boston Celtic star and NBA Hall of Famer, Bill Russell as host (along with the late Wayne Cody as co-host). Perryman's most controversial show which dealt with the subject, "homosexuality," resulted in an invitation from the gay community, asking Rev. Perryman to speak at their church. Perryman accepted their invitation and was the first heterosexual minister to deliver a sermon at the Metropolitan Community Church in Seattle, Washington. After his sermon, he received a standing ovation and hugs from the members of the gay congregation and criticism from local political and community leaders. Years later Perryman went to host "Let's Talk," another weekend talk show for singles on KCIS radio.

Perryman Researcher & Writer

In 1993, Rev. Perryman challenged major Christian publishers with his new research book entitled: The 1993 Trial on the Curse of Ham. The book provided proof that scholars were wrong when they stated that, according to the Bible *"the Black race was cursed"*. The curse theory was used to justify slavery, establish Jim Crow laws, and promote racial discrimination against African Americans. Perryman's research forced two major Christian publishers (Zondervan and Thomas Nelson) and the Encyclopedia Britannica to remove the curse theory from their publications. The theory had existed for over 500 years. In an article written by reporter, David Briggs of the Associated Press on February 17, 1995, he published the comments of Stanley N. Gundry, the Vice President and editor-in-chief of the book group for Zondervan. Gundry told the reporter, *"When Perryman called it to our attention, and pointed out how offensive it was to African - Americans, it was no big deal for us, we said, "Fine let's remove it."* Gundry went on to say that prior to Perryman's request, *"...there was nothing that would raise a flag for a Caucasian editor."* On October 26, 1994, publisher Thomas Nelson issued a letter stating: *"On behalf of our President, Sam Moore, I want to thank you for your letters and phone calls identifying errors in Nelson's Illustrated Bible Dictionary regarding "the curse of Ham.... Today, with the help of your communications and also of our relationships with an increasing number of African American scholars, editors and writers, we are more able to identify errors and blind spots...."* On November 11, 1994, Perryman received a similar letter of apology from the Encyclopedia Britannica. During that same year, Thomas Nelson (the nation's largest and oldest Christian publisher) asked Perryman to serve as their cultural/race adviser for their new upcoming Word of Life Study Bible and

Promise Keepers recruited him the train their regional managers in racial reconciliation.

In July 2009, Perryman's Commemorative Collector's Edition Post honoring President Lincoln for his 200th birthday became a permanent part of the Lincoln Presidential Library and Museum in Springfield, IL. The poster featured history not commonly known about Lincoln, along with his portrait, with a high quality gold-leaf and platinum design.

Perryman Unifying Black & White College Students

In 1995, Perryman received a frantic phone call from the president of Oral Roberts University. Racial tension at the university was at an all-time high and they needed someone to bring the campus together. The president indicated that a former student had recommended Rev. Perryman. After Perryman's visit, Professor Trevor Grizzle wrote: *"Dear Dr. Perryman: ...The deposit you left on the campus of Oral Roberts University continues to bear dividends. How can I begin to describe the far reaching effects of your sermons and talks to our students, staff, and faculty? No pen can tell. Suffice to say, you left behind a spirit of unity, a feeling of common brotherhood and sisterhood, an ambiance of goodwill. You have a way of disarming even the most hostile enemy, to walk in a minefield and defuse every landmine and leave a killing field a playground. In my thirteen years at this institution, no black speaker has spoken on the topics and issue you addressed and left the whole campus feeling the need to shake hands, repent of the sin of racism, embrace out of an awareness of filial consanguinity...."* Later, Dr. Grizzle, Rev. Perryman and several other African American scholars co-authored: the African Cultural Heritage Topical Bible. Perryman continues his work in the area of racial and cultural reconciliation as the President of **Humanity Diversity** LLC, an organization dedicated to healing the racial and cultural divide in America.

Perryman & National & International Recognition

Perryman, who was born and raised in the Seattle area (Bremerton, Washington April 30, 1945), is the author of a several books, film and a multitude of published articles. He has lectured from the west coast to the east coast, he has been a national featured speaker for many organizations and a guest on several radio and television shows during the past 40 years. On March 8, 1994, he had the honor of lecturing at the world-famous Mayo Clinic in Rochester, Minnesota. For his ongoing work as a servant to his community, Perryman has received a multitude of

9

commendations from the President of the United States, members of the United States Congress, and from former Washington State governor, Booth Gardner, former Seattle mayor, Charles Royer and community leaders.

In addition to this recognition, his selfless acts of compassion and service on behalf of others has been featured in local, national and international media organizations including Sports Illustrated Magazine, Sports Illustrated for Kids Magazine, Parade Magazine, Ebony Magazine, Upscale Magazine, Christianity Today Magazine, Charisma Magazines; the Seattle Times, ABC's Home Show, Fox's Hannity & Colmes, C-Span Book TV, TBN's 700 Club, the Tavis Smiley Show, the Michael Medved Show, the G.Gordon Liddy Show, Italy's Speak Up Magazine and a multitude of other publications and radio and television appearances.

Books & Film By Wayne Perryman

Children's Books: Children's Letters To God, What Mary Found, Hands to Love, Teddy Tyson's Terrible Feelings: **Books For Teens**: When Our Homes Had Porches, Teens & Young People Who Impacted The World – **Adult Books:** Affirmative Action Career Communicator, Kidnapped by Society, The African Heritage Cultural Topical Bible, 1993 Trial on The Curse of Ham, REAGA (on gangs), Unfounded Loyalty, Unveiling the Whole Truth, Drama of Obama, Whites Blacks & Racist Democrats, Why don't You Sing Me a Love Song, Thought Provoking Bible Studies of the 90's. Books currently ready for publishing include: Smoke Signals from a Pile of Leaves, Mr. Johnson's Apple Tree, and Skilled Professionals in Construction Industries. In 2014 Perryman, released his two-hour film documentary covering 395 years of Black History (from 1619-2014) entitled: "Because of The Color of Their Skin." In 1990, his 220 minute VHS management training series entitled: "Preventing Litigation in the Work Place," was released.

Father of Five

Wayne Perryman, born April 30, 1945 in Bremerton, Washington is the proud father of five children, Telisha Perryman, Latricia Perryman-Kinlow, Sean Perryman, Conner Perryman, and Dion Perryman (deceased). In 1979 he enrolled in City University majoring in business. He received his ministerial license from the Churches of God in Christ on April 28, 1974, under Bishop R.E. Altheimer and Presiding Bishop J. O. Patterson.

THOMAS NELSON PUBLISHERS
Nelson Place at Elm Hill Pike, P.O. Box 141000 Nashville, Tenn., 37214-1000

October 26, 1994

Rev. Wayne Perryman
Consultants Confidential
P.O. Box 256
Mercer Island, WA 98040

Dear Rev. Perryman:

On behalf of our President, Mr. Sam Moore, I want to thank you for your letters and phone calls identifying errors in NELSON'S ILLUSTRATED BIBLE DICTIONARY regarding "the curse of Ham."

I'm grateful that you already know that we are interested in correcting inaccuracies and in demonstrating sensitivity toward the feelings and interests of African Americans, who rightfully object to intentional racism and also to the harmful effects of mistakes that play into its ugly hand. Our interest is grounded in our desire to honor God and help advance His good purposes for all people through our products.

I hope it will please you to know that we are in the process of thoroughly revising NELSON'S ILLUSTRATED BIBLE DICTIONARY and are correcting errors in the specific entries you listed in your letter to Mark Roberts of March 25, 1994. I look forward to sending you a complimentary copy of NELSON'S NEW ILLUSTRATED BIBLE DICTIONARY upon its release, late spring 1995. Also, we are exercising care in our other publishing projects not only to avoid such outright errors, but also to avoid expressions from which some might draw unwarranted and racist inferences.

The original NELSON'S ILLUSTRATED BIBLE DICTIONARY was edited by the late Dr. Herbert Lockyer, Sr., who was apparently unaware of the issues you have raised. Today, with the help of your communications and also of our relationships with an increasing circle of African-American scholars, editors, and writers, we are more able to identify errors and blindspots of perception that need to be corrected and challenged so that our work testifies to the truth in love.

Again, thank you for challenging us to serve all of God's people without offense. We invite you to watch our response to these issues from here on and hope you will be pleased with our sincerity and progress.

Sincerely,

Philip P. Stoner
Vice President
Biblical & Religious Reference Publishing

cc: Hon. Andrew Young, Mr. Sam Moore

ENCYCLOPÆDIA BRITANNICA, INC.

Editorial Offices

November 11, 1994

The Rev. Wayne Perryman
President
Consultants Confidential
P.O. Box 256
Mercer Island, WA 98040

Dear Mr. Perryman:

Thank you for your recent comments concerning treatment in the encyclopaedia of biblical passages relating to Noah, Ham, and Canaan.

The Micropaedia entry "Noah" (3:737:2a), in a discussion of themes that have been traced in Genesis 9:20-27, states that during Noah's drunkenness, his son Ham acted disrespectfully toward him, whereupon Ham was cursed by Noah. As you noted, however, the passage in Genesis states that Noah placed a curse upon Canaan, and not Ham. The *Britannica* entry will be amended in this regard as soon as our revision schedule permits.

The *Britannica* entry also states that the above passage may have been used as a veiled justification for the subjection of the Canaanites by the Israelites. Certainly, most scholars acknowledge this possibility, and we have no plans to delete this information from the entry. Other sources have noted that historically, the passage has been cited--however inappropriately--as evidence in favor of the enslavement or degradation of people of African descent. It is our belief that neither the biblical text in question, nor its treatment in the *Encyclopaedia Britannica*, could be logically used to support such a claim.

Thank you for having taken the time to comment.

Sincerely yours,

Stephen P. Davis
Editorial Division

BRITANNICA CENTRE

≜ ZondervanPublishingHouse

January 20, 1995

Rev. Wayne Perryman, President
Consultants Confidential
P.O. Box 256
Mercer Island, WA 98040

Dear Wayne:

Please excuse the tardiness of my reply to our correspondence and discussions of last October.
However, I believe that I warned you that the next couple of months were exceedingly busy
for me and that it would be some time before I could get back to you with a more official
indication of our decision with regard to the "Curse of Ham" sections in several books that you
called to our attention.

In this more formal way I want to notify you that I have taken steps to make the necessary
corrections, removing the "Curse of Ham" interpretation from the titles that you mentioned,
and revising the text to more faithfully reflect what the Genesis 9 passage actually says.

I went beyond the information that you gave me and, just as I suspected, found several other
titles that also had this interpretation in them. However, these additional titles were simply
earlier editions of the same works that you had mentioned to me. So far as I know, this
completely removes this interpretation from any Zondervan products. The titles that will be
corrected in their next printings are:

Nave's Compact Topical Bible
The Nave's Topical Bible
The NIV Compact Nave's Topical Bible
The Zondervan NIV Nave's Topical Bible
Commentary on the Whole Bible by Matthew Henry, edited by Leslie F. Church
The NIV Matthew Henry Commentary in One Volume, revising editor Gerald W. Peterman.

I trust you understand that most of these titles have a number of months of inventory
remaining in our warehouse, and there are even more books that are in the "pipeline" with
distributors and bookstores around the country. So, it could be a number of months, maybe
even a year or two before the pipeline is completely cleared of the old editions.

Rooted in history, grounded in faith, moving forward to serve the world

Rev. Wayne Perryman
Page 2

But as I indicated above, I am taking steps immediately to make sure that corrections are made to the appropriate page of each volume so that when we go to the next printing we will be ready with the corrected text.

Cordially,

Stanley N. Gundry
Vice President and Editor-in-Chief
Book Group

pjw

ASSOCIATE PRESS

A,L,9 – BC-FEA BIBLE –CURSE   02-16 0634
BC-FEA—Bible Curse, 0647
Testaments 2-17

Minister Seeks to Lift the Curse of Ham

By David Briggs
AP Religion Writer

"Curse be Canaan, lowest of slaves she he be to his brothers," Noah say after being discovered drunk and naked in his tent.

Yet from this passage in the Book of Genesis somehow emerged the infamous Curse of Ham – the theory that Noah cursed Ham instead of Canaan.

Since Ham is often the father of the black race, the passage has at time been used to justify generation of oppression endured by blacks under slavery or colonialism, or to explain away their unequal treatment in more recent times.

Even if the idea is rejected in contemporary biblical scholarship, it endures in the backs of the minds of many black and white churchgoers, says a Seattle minister campaigning to remove the last vestiges of the curse of Ham from churches and scholarly works.

The Rev. Wayne Perryman, author of The 1993 Trial On The Curse of Ham, says major publishers such as Thomas Nelson and the Encyclopedia Britannica have agreed to make clear in future editions of books that refer to the curse, that is was Ham's son Canaan – not Ham – on whom the curse was placed.

Last month, Zondervan Publishing House agreed to remove the curse of Ham interpretation from future editions of six of its titles, including The Nave's Topical Bible and Commentary of the Whole Bible by Matthew Henry.

"I only hope that other publishers will follow in their footsteps," said Perryman, an associate minister of the Mount Calvary Church of God In Christ in Seattle. "Acknowledging wrongdoing and embracing what is right is the only way true reconciliation between blacks and whites in America can happen."

In the biblical account in Genesis 9, Noah becomes drunk from wine and lies uncovered in his tent. Ham sees his father nakedness, which was considered sinful in the culture at the time and tells his two brothers. The brothers avert their eyes and cover Noah. When Noah wakes up from his drunken sleep, he curses Canaan, the son of Ham.

The transfer by later interpreters of the curse from Canaan to Ham has no basis in either the biblical text or early Jewish thought, according to the Anchor Bible Dictionary.

The popular expression the curse of Ham is also not found in post-biblical Jewish literature.

The New Revised Standard version of The New Oxford Annotated Bible says in its note on the passage that since the curse was put on Canaan, it is likely that Canaan was the one who saw Noah' nakedness. It also note that the curse that the curse implies Canaan' subjugation to Israel was the result of Canaanite sexual practices.

However, despite the objections of the scholars throughout history, since it was considered wrong for Ham to observe and report on his father's nakedness, the traidtion somehow developed that the curse was placed on Ham.

Misplacing the curse on Ham, whose name is associated with the Egyptian name for ancient Egypt "the black land," contributed to the later justification of slavery and colonialism, according to the Anchor Dictionary.

Still today, the idea that the problems and unequal treatment black people face are somehow a result of the curse of Ham persists in different forms, Perryman says. He commended the publishers for making the changes.

Stanley N. Gundry, vice president and editor –in-chief of the book group at Zondervan, said the curse of Ham was found only in older works that were being reprinted, and there was nothing that would raise a red flag for a Caucasian editor.

"When Perryman called it to our attention, and pointed out how offensive it was to African-Americans, it was no big deal for us, We said, Fine let's eliminate it."

AP-WS-02-17-95 0733EST

ORAL ROBERTS
UNIVERSITY

February 13, 1995

Rev. Dr. Wayne Perryman, President
Consultants Confidential Inc.
P.O. Box 256
Mercer Island, WA 98040

Dear Dr. Perryman:

May the peace of our Lord be with you!

What this dilatory correspondence fails to accomplish
palliating my stinging conscience I hope your Christian
graciousness and understanding will do. It is to your Christian
magnanimity that I now appeal, for only that can absolve me of my
most terrible sin of procrastination - a procrastination that
results not from ethical inertia or entrepreneurial ineptitude
but the press of schedule and the scarcity of time.

While respecting due protocol and without presuming upon our
brief preliminary encounter, I want to say I feel a kindred
spirit with you. So winsome is your personality, so affable your
disposition - graces that waft a fragrance sweet. Yet lest such
sterling qualities be misconstrued as moral incivility, there
runs a strength of character, a resoluteness of will so
indomitable that none can mistake.

Meeting you was a breath of fresh air. The deposit you left
on the campus of Oral Roberts University continues to bear
dividend. How can I begin to describe the far reaching effects
of your sermons and talks to our students, staff, and faculty?
No pen can tell. Suffice it to say, you left behind you a spirit
of unity, a feeling of common brotherhood and sisterhood, an
ambiance of goodwill. You have a way of disarming even the most
hostile enemy, to walk in a minefield and defuse every landmine
and leave a killing field a playground. In my thirteen years at
this institution, no black speaker has spoken on the topics and
issues you addressed and left the whole campus feeling the need
to shake hands, repent of the sin of racism, embrace out of an
awareness of filial consanguinity. Thanks. I hope the Lord will
so choreograph your travels as to bring you back here - and soon!

Accept my personal thanks for your work titled Thought
Provoking Bible Studies. I have already consumed much of its
contents. Brilliant! I applaud your fecund mind, energetic pen,

and inexhaustible resourcefulness. What a force for the Kingdom you are!

I would like you to send me a price list of your published works. Too, if my request does not fall outside the bounds of propriety, I would deeply appreciate copies of your marvelous poems.

What great privilege it has been meeting you. I hope our acquaintance will broaden and deepen over the years. It may be more than fortuitous happenstance that Mr. Derwyn Stewart of Pneuma Life Publisher has us contributing to The African Cultural Heritage Bible due out next month. I have enclosed a copy of the Introduction I have written for your perusal.

May God continue to bless you in all your endeavors.

Sincerely in Christ,

Trevor Grizzle

Trevor Grizzle, Ph.D.
Associate Professor of New Testament
Graduate School of Theology
Oral Roberts University

1/19/2018   RE: Photo of Police Training

From: Scott Behrbaum <ScottB@issaquahwa.gov>
To: 'doublebro@aol.com' <doublebro@aol.com>
Subject: RE: Photo of Police Training
Date: Wed, Sep 28, 2016 1:15 pm
Attachments: 20160922_140643.jpg (5466K), 20160922_140647.jpg (5657K), 20160922_140639.jpg (5602K)

Wayne

Thank you for coming to talk with our departments. It was an opportune time for us to have your presentation and continue the discussion about what our communities are experiencing. I have received numerous compliments on your discussion points, and there have been continued conversations within the department. One of our original goals of your presentation was to educate and hopefully draw out deeper discussions and thought. This was definitely accomplished.

I am working on the printed version of the pic and will get it too you soon.

Scott

Scott Behrbaum | Chief of Police
Issaquah Police Department
130 E. Sunset Way | PO BOX 1307 | Issaquah, WA 98027
425-837-3216 (desk) | 425-864-6211 (cell) | www.issaquahwa.gov

From: doublebro@aol.com [mailto:doublebro@aol.com]
Sent: Wednesday, September 28, 2016 9:27 AM
To: Scott Behrbaum
Subject: Photo of Police Training

Chief Scott

When you get a chance, can you send me a copy of the group photo that we took at the training session. I would not only like a copy for my website via e-mail, but a hard copy as well.

It was great working with you, you are a class act and an outstanding professional. Your staff is blessed to have a chief like you.

Wayne Perryman
Humanity Diversity
P.O. Box 256
Mercer Island, WA 98040
(206) 708-6676

  3 Attached Images

https://mail.aol.com/webmail-std/en-us/PrintMessage   1/

Special Thanks

I want to thank my sons, Conner and Sean, my daughters: Telisha and Latricia and my friends: Doris, Robert, George, Frankie Vena and former Seahawk and 49ers, Charlie Young for their love, support, prayers and encouragement.